Manifesting
Miracles

True Stories of Extraordinary
Coincidences

BARBARA E. HARRIS

MANIFESTING MIRACLES

True Stories of Extraordinary Coincidences

By Barbara E. Harris

Transcendent Publishing
PO Box 66202
St. Pete Beach, FL 33736
www.TranscendentPublishing.com

ISBN: 978-0-9600501-7-8
Library of Congress Control Number: 2019905617

Printed in the United States of America.

DEDICATION

*T*his book is dedicated to my daughter-in-love, Amy, who has steadfastly believed in my spiritual gifts and encouraged me to write this book. Amy is also the living personification of having Faith when walking through the fire. Her own medical challenges, as well as those of her husband and their three sons, would have devastated most. Instead, these challenges brought her to her knees and increased her Faith in God. She is an example for us all.

I thank my son, Randy, for all he has done to live as a devoted husband and father during these times of trial, as well as a humble, successful businessman and Christian. Thank you for bringing Amy, a Blessed Earth Angel, into my life over forty years ago.

I thank you both for loving me and teaching me what is important in life. May you be forever blessed.

Love,

Mom

ACKNOWLEDGEMENTS

*M*y gratitude to all who appear in this book, though names, places and minor details have been changed to protect their anonymity.

I credit my mother, Ethel Moore Van Splinter, for my steadfast Faith and belief in things unknown, and my beloved Aunt "Mamie" Moore for my positive, generous spirit. Mamie taught me to accept both joy and sorrow with Grace. She also taught me that Beauty lies within. For that and for all the memorable moments we shared I am forever grateful.

A special thank you to the friends who always believed in the special gifts given to me. Your enthusiasm, encouragement and support have been immeasurable during this long journey. You are too numerous to name, but you know who you are. I thank you from the bottom of my heart.

To Marty H., my computer guru, who converted the discs of my first book into a Word document, without which I would not have started this book. To Ros Petti, a fellow author who encouraged me to join *The Spiritual Writer's Network* and submit my poetry and short stories for publication. Without that nudge to get started writing again I doubt this book would have manifested. Praise and gratitude to Shanda Trofe of Transcendent Publishing, my writing coach and publisher as well as a talented teacher of the many facets of book publishing.

For my dearest friend, Barbara, who always encouraged me to write poetry and this book. I shall always cherish you and the love of your life, Bill.

And to Paul (his nom de plume), who constantly asks "Did you write today?" and "Keep writing, Bobbi." I am so grateful that he is in my life.

To the Live Poet's Society members Sara, Katherine, Shelley, Judy and Mike, who teach me with their kind critiques and unfailing grace—thank you for believing in my poetry.

Most of all, I am eternally grateful for the gifts God gave me to write both poetry and prose, and for those responsible for the tales of synchronicity, be they Angels, Spirit or a yet unknown phenomena... my words alone cannot express my gratitude. Thank you, God, for creating this wonderful, mysterious Universe.

CONTENTS

FOREWORD

These are the words of my late husband, Linton I. (Chip) Harris, written for my previous book now out of print. They are just as relevant to the stories chronicled in this book, which Chip also witnessed until his untimely death on September 26, 2015.

"When I find myself in times of trouble, Mother Mary comes to me." Although these words were written by John Lennon in 1970, they could have been written by my wife, Barbara Harris. *Manifesting Miracles: True Stories of Extraordinary Coincidences* is a book that contains compelling accounts of mystical, spiritual events.

I worked many years in the left-brain world for a large corporation. My marriage to "Bobbi" twenty-three* years ago started me on a path that led to the magic of unexplainable synchronous events in my own life. This journey accelerated following a successful bout with cancer and ultimately led to a position as an interfaith hospital chaplain. It was while serving the dying and their families that my own spiritual experiences reached a pinnacle. I am now able to understand

---

* When I wrote this book it had been forty-two years since our wedding.

and appreciate the events related in this book to which I was a witness and participant.

It has taken much courage for Bobbi to write this book. I watched as she struggled *not to write* some of the words that seemed to be "sent" to her. Yet in the end she achieved the telling of a miraculous and unusual life story. The theme of Mary as the Universal Mother and a call for a return to caring and compassion are more than evident. I recommend this book to people of all religions and faiths as a book about unconditional love.

Linton (Chip) I. Harris Dr. RS., MBA, BSEE 1934-2015

INTRODUCTION

*W*hat is Synchronicity? According to renowned psychologist Dr. Carl Jung, it is a "meaningful coincidence"—an ironic choice of words considering Jung, who coined the term, believed there were no accidents.

Synchronicity, he contended, is the occurrence of simultaneous events that are related in a profound yet *a causal* way. These events *align to the personal concerns or thoughts* of the individual. An example of this would be when you think of an old friend with whom you have not spoken for a long time and she suddenly calls you.

> *"Synchronicity is an ever-present reality for those who have eyes to see"*
>
> *~Dr. Carl Jung*

I have always been aware of the many synchronicities or extraordinary coincidences occurring in my life; in fact, I wisely recorded them before they were forgotten. These events have had a profound effect on my life. They caused me to wonder what it all means, which in turn led me to read books about quantum physics. Still, the questions remain. How do these extraordinary "coincidences" occur?

I know there are many healthy skeptics out there and I count myself among them. We are those people who are highly aware and whose consciousness is raised. We question the whys and hows of what seems to be magic!

I know it is difficult to believe in a phenomenon that cannot be explained. It is perhaps due to the fear of a mysterious, hidden world. I respectfully ask that you read my book with an open mind, for if you become aware you will almost certainly begin to notice the synchronicities, the coincidences and the magic in your own life.

For me now there is no fear, for I have traveled to the other side during a Near Death Experience (NDE) and know there is a paradigm beyond the physical. There is actually a feeling of amazement, wonder, and euphoria when these unexplainable experiences happen.

I still have questions and often ask myself why these things are happening to me? I've come to understand that they happen to everyone; it is simply because my consciousness has been raised and I am now very aware. I also have the luxury of time to go within and listen to the inner voice.

Whatever the Truth is, I do believe that synchronicity is more than just a coincidence; for me it is Magic…it is Divine Providence in Action, guiding my life.

"The day science begins to study non-physical phenomena, it will make more progress in one decade than in all the previous centuries of its existence."

~ Nikola Tesla

In the pages that follow, I present my experiences and leave it to you to evaluate the odds of them unfolding the way they did.

Blessings,

Bobbi

"Coincidence is the language of the stars. For something to happen, so many forces have to be put into action."

~ Paulo Coelho

Chapter One

THE EARLIEST MANIFESTATIONS

O ne of the earliest signs of an unexpected event happened when I was seventeen years of age. I was called into the Guidance Director's office at my high school and informed that I had received a full scholarship to a nursing school. I sat there, stunned, as I had not applied for a nursing scholarship, or to a nursing school, for that matter! After college I had planned on attending medical school; I wanted to be a doctor so I could heal people.

God knew something I did not. Medical students did not focus on healing, but spent much of their time dissecting cadavers and studying hard-wired, Newtonian-based science. Nurses, on the other hand, had a lot more time and opportunities to be with the patient than physicians. Yes, the doctors could prescribe medications, but it was the nurse that provided the tender loving care, the touch and the hope. It was the nurse who spent the hours with the sick and the dying. It was the nurse who promoted not simply "curing", but healing! And it was true that healing often ended with the death of the physical body.

As committed as I was to my dream, it was the early fifties, a time when there were few women physicians. In fact, my twin brother had already been designated by my mother to be the future doctor in the family. Realizing that a nursing education was as close as I was going to get to medicine, I accepted the scholarship. It was quite a surprise, as I had never pictured myself as a nurse.

As it turned out, nursing provided me with the knowledge I could never have achieved in medical school. Though I did not know it at the time, this was my first lesson in "not outlining the outcome."

It was also, unbeknownst to me, my first lesson in manifesting. There was an unseen force—which I call *Spirit* or *God*—who knew nursing would be the path through which my desire to heal would be attained. That force had presented me with an opportunity, and my acceptance of it would change and influence the rest of my life.

That summer after graduation was spent in continuing my work in an insurance agency. I was now a full-time employee and earning what to me was a fortune, yet now I chose to give up the income for my education. It would not be the last time I would do that.

My new journey became real when "out of the blue" I was called for an appointment with the Dean of the Nursing Program to review my scores given by the National League of Nursing admissions test.

I shall never forget how elegant the director looked that day. Her white hair was neatly coiffed in a bun that matched her starched, high-necked white uniform. Each long sleeve had at least twenty small buttons, and as I sat across from her I couldn't help wondering, *How in the world did she ever get those things fastened?* I would have my answer three years later when I graduated from the program.

But that day seemed light years away as I sat, with my

mother by my side, discussing the results of a test I barely remembered taking. The director was telling me that I had scored near the top in the country in Ancient History! That struck me as odd, as I had never studied the subject.

She questioned me about my reading of this history…but there was none. I did not think anything of it at the time. It would be much later, when I was reading about past lives and underwent past life regressions by a clinical psychologist that I began to develop a theory about my aptitude for history.

After being accepted into this School of Nursing my left brain was called into action as I studied the sciences. Anatomy, Physiology, Chemistry, and Microbiology were now filling every cell in my brain. The challenge was to get through the first six "probie" months to earn a cap!

When we were not sitting in lectures or cracking open textbooks, my fellow students and I were working in the hospital, our introduction to the Art of Nursing. It was a rigorous schedule that I enjoyed; at last my potential to learn was being tapped! This was a sharp contrast from grammar and high school, which I sailed through with little to no studying. It made my knowledge of history on the test all the more curious and would now fuel my quest to learn it.

It would not be until much later, when I was a Registered Nurse, that another piece of the puzzle slid into place. I was working in the operating room as a scrub nurse, assisting the surgeons. This was an invitation-only position, and I was honored to be asked to serve with this close-knit group under a tough but fair director. I also loved the work.

One day, the Chief of Surgery, who was my favorite

doctor to work with, said to me and my friend Millie, "Hey, you kids! (Millie and I were twenty-one years old) I have two Broadway tickets to *The Lark* starring Julie Harris for Friday night … front orchestra seats … would you want to use them? My wife is sick and we can't go."

Would we!! I had no idea what the play was about or who Julie Harris, the lead actress, was, but it didn't matter. Millie and I were both in serious relationships with interns whom we would later marry. On their grand salary of twenty-five dollars a week they certainly couldn't afford to take us to a Broadway play.

That Friday, as we headed toward the bright lights on Broadway, I had no idea I was about to have a profound experience. When I learned the play was about the life of Joan of Arc, I didn't think much of it … at least not until the end, when she was tied to the stake and burned. The fire flickering at her feet and licking her legs was torturous for me to watch. Her accompanying screams, acted superbly by Julie Harris, were more than I could bear.

I remained very poised but tears streamed down my face and the hair on my arms stood up; incredible chills traveled up my spine. I had the vague sensation that I had once been burned at a stake, but quickly dismissed the thought as absurd. I remember saying to Millie, "I have chills from her screams!" and her response, "Yes, she is a great actress." We did not discuss it any further, nor did I discuss it with anyone else at that time.

Later I would recall another clue to the new perceptions and the world that would open up to me. It was back in nursing school, when my colleagues and I were living in student housing. Seeking a break from our grueling schedules, a group of us would gather in the lounge to chat and sing songs. I always initiated the same song: "I'm a Ramblin' Wreck from Georgia Tech and a Hell of an Engineer." I did not know how I knew it or why I sang it.

Little did I know that my second husband and my stepdaughter would be graduates of Georgia Tech, or that I would one day have a grandson at the time of this writing who is majoring in neuroscience there. Perhaps he will someday discover the secret to the stories that I am about to share.

I look back now and realize that these were signs of God tapping me on the shoulder perhaps trying to raise my awareness and consciousness … but I was not ready.

It would take major events to get my attention. When they occurred, it was both scary and divine and left me awestruck. It touched me at the deepest spiritual level. I could not explain the magnitude of what I was experiencing, yet somehow, I knew I would never be the same. Nothing, however, could prepare me for what was to come.

"... there are only two symptoms of enlightenment, just two indications that a transformation is taking place within you toward a higher consciousness. The first symptom is that you stop worrying. Things don't bother you anymore. You become light-hearted and full of joy. The second symptom is that you encounter more and more meaningful coincidences in your life, more and more synchronicities. And this accelerates to the point where you actually experience the miraculous."

~ Carol Lynn Pearson, Consider the Butterfly

Chapter Two

MANIFESTATION OF MOTHER MARY

*D*ear *Mother Mary,* I prayed fervently, *will you protect me if I publish my stories?*

Don't be afraid, my child, she replied, *Tell your stories.*

Please send me a sign, I pleaded. *It has been years since you appeared to me. Won't you please come again?*

Just a few days later, while watching the evening news, I was astonished to hear the following report:

"Scientists are still searching for an earthly explanation for the forty-foot image resembling the Madonna that appeared on nine sections of a smoked glass window in the Seminole Finance Building on December 17th."

I stood in the family room and watched, stunned, as television cameras swept over the thousands of visitors gathered that evening. Just a few days earlier I had asked Mother Mary for a sign. Steady, I thought. Don't let your imagination run away with you. Yet there I stood, motionless, as if glued to the spot.

The reporter continued with amazement in his voice. "According to the Associated Press, the infirm, the faithful, and the hopeful—nearly half a million of them—have flocked to Clearwater, Florida on this week before Christmas to see this image. The building's owner has no explanation for it, but he acknowledges that an incredible artist and divine intervention must have played a part in creating this glorious image of the Virgin Mary."

Hearing this broadcast took my breath away. My hands began to tremble and my heartbeat quickened. In just a few days, my husband Chip and I would be having Christmas Day dinner with my son Erick and his family in Palm Harbor, just a few short miles from the Clearwater building. The fact that a visit to the site of the image would be a convenient side trip did not escape my notice. Was this a mere coincidence, or one of those synchronous events Carl Jung theorized about?

Could this image of the Mother Mary be a demonstration for me? Can my stories be so important to mankind that the Blessed Mother has made this appearance?

"I don't think so!" I said out loud with certainty, and yet my excitement and curiosity increased at the mere thought of going to Clearwater.

I had always had a rather special, comforting relationship with the Blessed Mother Mary, the genesis of which was a bit of a mystery. Neither the Baptist church I attended for the first twelve years of my life nor the small neighborhood Methodist church I belonged to thereafter emphasized Mary's role. I certainly was aware that Mary was the mother of Jesus, and I do remember saying "born of the Virgin Mary" during the Apostles' Creed spoken on Sunday mornings. However, her role was minor compared to the revered status she holds in the Roman Catholic Church.

Suddenly a clear, sweet memory came to mind. I was a

little girl of about three years old, and it was Christmastime. I picked up a statuette of Mary from my aunt's beautiful manger and kissed it. I did not want to let it go and the adults had to pry it out of my hands. Odd that I remembered that incident these many years later! I wondered if my soul had been hinting at the depth of the relationship I would one day have with Mother Mary.

That evening I tentatively broached the subject of going to Clearwater with Chip I told him about the people claiming the appearance to be a vision of Mary and learned that he had already heard about it on the car radio. I then asked him if he knew where the building was located and was amazed when he readily produced a map and showed me the spot. In fact, he had already considered the possibility of a visit. I was very surprised that he had an interest in seeing the image.

I did not say anything to him about my prayer and its possible connection to Mother Mary as I thought he would think it ludicrous. Nor did I tell our youngest daughter, Amy, who was visiting for the holidays and would accompany us on the journey.

On Christmas Day we drove along U.S. 19 toward the finance building. The traffic was flowing normally, then suddenly slowed to a crawl as we approached the building. As we inched forward, I lowered the car window hoping to get a glimpse of the building or the window. I saw nothing. Then the pace quickened. Adrenaline surged through me as a traffic cop stopped our car to allow streams of people to cross the highway. He grinned at us through the windshield, and my husband rolled down his window.

"Merry Christmas!" Chip called. "Quite a crowd, eh?"

"It's unbelievable," the young officer said, laughing. "We're expecting twenty-five thousand people here today."

We parked the car in a large lot across the street, then joined the throng at the side of the building, where thousands of people could gather at one time. Awestruck crowds were staring up at the immense darkened window brought alive with the rainbow image of the Blessed Mother Mary. I was unprepared for the rush of emotions I experienced. For me, this image required neither faith nor imagination to look like the Madonna. It was not a shapeless form. Brilliant sunlight, streaming across the nine, large-paned windows, clearly outlined the motherly figure in luminous color. I was astonished, and the sanctity of the moment took my breath away.

For days the newscasters had been treating the vision lightly, but not one scientist had yet been able to explain the formation of this heavenly shape. It was thought that minerals in the water had created the distinct silhouette, but how? Had the mineral, water, and glass experts come forward? I wondered.

All around me, reverently silent children and adults knelt on the asphalt. Some made the sign of the cross over their tattered T-shirts or exquisite holiday finery. Most people clasped rosary beads in hopeful hands. I became extremely aware that I was not a Roman Catholic and also acutely aware of the importance of Mother Mary in the lives of others. Then the thought came to me that I did not have to be Roman Catholic to honor Mother Mary as the Universal Mother.

The melodious sounds of Spanish, French, and Italian blended beautifully with crisp New England and soft Southern accents. Metal wheelchairs and wooden crutches intermingled with exquisite emeralds and dazzling diamonds. No one seemed conscious of status or apparel. We were the people of faith and hope, all coming together this Christmas Day in this spiritual moment—all believing in the unseen side of life. We were all one!

I peered ahead to a makeshift altar where candles of all colors and shapes flickered dimly in the bright sunlight. Nearby, on a drab, gray concrete wall in front of the windows, an ordinary, small cardboard box held donations for All Children's Hospital in St. Petersburg, Florida. Single roses, pink and red, and small bouquets of brightly colored flowers—some plastic—were scattered on the wall. A red poinsettia or two were casually placed on the ground.

The holiness and reverence of the moment were palpable in the air. Yet as I looked up at the image, I was stunned by my reaction. My breath was momentarily taken away, my heart began to beat rapidly, and the hair on my arms stood up straight. An icy chill ran up my spine as I stood transfixed. I consciously centered myself and took some deep breaths. *Now don't get carried away,* my objective self said, *Look at this rationally.*

Suddenly, I heard Mother Mary's nurturing voice reverberating in my heart. It was as if a tape recorder had been turned on. The clarity and sweetness of the sound took me by surprise.

"It has been said that I would come and give messages to the planet," she said. "I have come to Clearwater, Florida, because the name of the city is significant. This is an important part of my message. You must have clear water. The pollution of the water must stop. This is not an option. This is necessary for the survival of the planet. The seas and the oceans are your lifeline.

"It is no coincidence that you are here this day," the blessed voice continued, "I have chosen you as a vehicle through whom my message will be spread. For many months you have been debating whether to accept this assignment. This is my last call to you. You must tell of this day and of our previous meetings in a book."

In that sacred moment, my heart overflowed with love. My eyes brimming full with tears, now spilled unabashedly over onto my winter-tanned cheeks. I looked up at the Blessed Mother and silently said, *Oh, Mother Mary, I don't know whether I have the courage to tell of our hallowed meetings. I am so afraid of ridicule.*

"Yes, tell your stories," she lovingly urged. "Let it be known unto all the people, for they are stories about the sacredness of all life. This is not a question of religion. Those are man-made—it is a question of faith and souls being denied access to the body. All individuals must be responsible for their actions. To do otherwise is to wreak havoc on the earth. You must tell of the miracles of birth and the choice of adoption. This is my message to you: Put forth your book for all whose eyes are open to see."

And just like that the voice fell silent, leaving me overwhelmed and awestruck. *Me, write a book?* I did not know how to write a book. Who would publish it if I wrote it? But deep in my soul I knew I would obey her mandate.

As we left the building and headed to Erick's, I tried to behave as if nothing unusual had happened. Though I was bursting at the seams, I said nothing to my family for fear that the sacredness of the moment and Mother's Mary's message might be lost in telling of it.

My resolve didn't last long, however. When we returned home that evening, I recorded her message to the best of my recollection and shared it with my husband. Although he was an engineer and computer scientist by education, he had been led into a hospital chaplain's training program following a bout with cancer. And, after nearly a quarter century of marriage, he was now accustomed to my frequent intuitive experiences and was encountering synchronicity in his own life.

"Something extraordinary happened to me at Clearwater," I began hesitantly, then recounted my experience with Mother Mary, including the strong directive she had given me while standing in front of the window. "She told me to write a book about her visits to me through the years," I added.

Chip's response was nonchalant but supportive. "That sounds interesting. It would be quite an undertaking. I accept the stories because I was there, but are you sure you want to publicly go out on a limb like that?"

"If I don't crawl out on a limb, how can I taste the fruit?" I replied, rather annoyed. "I don't know what to do." I wasn't sure I could write the stories, or if I even wished to share them with the world, yet when I spoke again my voice was suddenly filled with bravado. "Mother Mary told me to write the book, so I have to trust that I will be shown the way!"

For years I had suppressed the extraordinary events surrounding my NDE and the adoptions of one daughter and the surrendering of a grandson to another. My rational mind warned me to keep my secrets, and the prospect of going public upset me because privacy—my own and my two daughters was of the utmost importance to me. After receiving Mother Mary's mandate, however, I realized I had no choice. After all, she had played a major part in guiding both adoptions and two hospitalizations. I could no longer deny the role she had played in my life. I obtained permission from my daughters to tell their adoption stories. Nothing stood in my way now but my fear of disclosure.

In the next few months, my life slowly changed. I saw fewer friends and spent more time in prayer and contemplation. Our social life dwindled to almost nothing. I began to sit at the computer to write about my experiences with Mother Mary.

It was a challenging process to say the least. I had always intensely disliked technological devices, and even more so now that my husband had installed a new software program on our computer. I did not know how to use it and was often very frustrated and unable to work when he was not home to answer my questions. Soon, the very idea of sitting before that screen brought up feelings of dread, and my stories remained unread and unedited for weeks at a time. The task of writing a book had always been formidable; now it seemed insurmountable.

The more I wanted to escape it, the more the book invaded my life. My growing fear about going public—and being considered delusional—manifested as bad dreams. There were also reminders while tending to my busy private holistic nursing practice. I arrived at the home of a client – the first I agreed to see for such a visit – to see an exquisite oil painting of the Virgin Mary hanging over her bed. Two paintings of ethereal angels flanked the central painting. It turned out the woman, a talented musical director, had brought the paintings from Italy where she had conducted a choir for the pope.

My client asked me to visit her dear friend, who was also very ill. It turned out the friend had three adopted children. More synchronicity! It seemed Mother Mary was not going to let me escape her message so easily. The burning desire, the nagging voice, the constant knowing that I must write, would not go away, and yet still the stories remained untouched.

A full year would pass before any news of the Madonna of the Window, as I now called her, was sent my way. A friend called to tell me about an article she had seen in the Venice Gondolier, a small Florida newspaper.

"Say, didn't you tell me that you and Chip went to see the image of Mary in Clearwater?" she asked.

"Yes, we did," I answered.

She mentioned the article and said she was going to send it to me.

"Oh, thanks," I replied, trying not to sound too eager, "Sounds interesting."

In truth, I could not wait to see what the story said.

My excitement would soon turn to disappointment. According to the newspaper, the building had been leased as office space to a company called *Ugly Duckling Car Sales*. I didn't like the name and tried to look past it for some deeper meaning. Perhaps there was a connection to the children's story; perhaps, like the ugly duckling, this vision of Mary was in its infancy and would mature into an international shrine for her. I prayed this would happen.

The rest of the article was even less encouraging. Apparently, scientists were now saying that the discoloration in the glass panes was caused by a chemical reaction from the watering of shrubbery! I of course was not satisfied with the explanation. If it had been a chemical reaction, why hadn't it also occurred on the windows on the other sides of the building? How was it possible for the distinct pattern to continue between the large panes that reached up more than forty feet, and how had it been forever embedded in the panes? How did the water *reach* a height of forty feet in the first place? The scientists had not explained any of those things.

The most fascinating—and perhaps most disturbing—piece of information in the article was about a Fort Lauderdale stockbroker who thought the image to be a statement about abortion. Reading that, I got a chill and the hair on my arms stood up. He pointed out that the Virgin image appears on nine panes of glass, each representing a month of pregnancy. He further stated that the image faced the abortion clinic that was just a mile down the street. I sure did not want to get embroiled in that controversy!

Despite its disheartening tone, I still felt the article was a nudge from Mother Mary, a reminder that her message to me a full year earlier was even more valid and important. It now seemed imperative that I complete my book. My determination intensified and I made plans to close my practice to free up the time I needed.

In the years since Mary's appearance there have been several updates on this holy site:

St. Petersburg Times, 2004

CLEARWATER, Fla. (AP) -- Office building windows that thousands of visitors believed bore the image of the Virgin Mary were discovered broken Monday, police said.

The three top panes that showed what appeared to be the Virgin Mary's veiled head were destroyed, with just shards of glass remaining in the window frames. The damage was discovered when a ministry worker arrived Monday morning and it is believed the damage was done overnight, police spokesman Wayne Shelor said.

Investigators were trying to determine how the windows were broken.

The image first appeared a week before Christmas in 1996 in what was then a home finance office, drawing almost 500,000 visitors within weeks.

Stretching almost 60 feet high and more than 20 feet across on nine bronze-colored glass panels, the image was evocative of a stained-glass portrait of Mary. Shades of purple, blue, yellow and green washed across the mirrored surface and swirled into a robe-draped figure with downcast head.

Glass experts believe the image was created by a chemical reaction and corrosion of the metallic elements in the glass coating, but they could not explain why it took the shape it did.

So many pilgrims came to the site that extra police patrols were in place for a time. The office building later became the home of Ohio-based Shepherds of Christ Ministries.

Six months after the apparition first drew worldwide attention, someone threw an undetermined liquid on the shape, marring it. But after two days of heavy thunderstorms, the blemishes were no longer visible.

Vandals Destroy Head of Miracle Virgin Mary Image

Vandals shattered the office building glass that made up part of a 60-ft. tall apparition of the Virgin Mary in Clearwater, Florida on March 1. Unknown assailants took out the top three panels of glass, which made up the veil and face of the Virgin Mary, with a slingshot and three ball bearings.

Authorities are studying a tape from a surveillance camera but haven't said if they've found anything on it yet.

The oily image of Mary first appeared in 1996 and has drawn a steady audience of believers and onlookers ever since. The miracle has recovered from vandals before (someone tossed acid on it a while back, but the image reappeared). "It may be tougher this time."

[03/07/2004] ROADSIDE AMERICA

High School Kid Admits Slingshot Assault on Virgin Mary Windows.

A high school sophomore in Clearwater, Florida, admitted to police he fired ball bearings with a Marksman slingshot that destroyed the image of the Virgin Mary in an office building window. The 60-ft. tall oily image appeared miraculously in 1996 and has been the focus of visits by believers and the curious. The attack took place on March 1, 2004, destroying the top three panes of glass. Information received last week led investigators to question 18-year old Kyle Maskell. Maskell, an angry teenager driven by guilt to confess, said he was sorry.

Update: July 13, 2004 - Downey jailed Maskell for 10 days and ordered him to pay the ministry $1,200 for the damage. The owners of the building didn't want to press charges, but apparently the attorney general did.

2005: Apparently part of the image remains. In January, the building owners installed bulletproof glass over the whole thing to prevent another incident.

June of 2018: while writing this book I found another update on Facebook. The woman who posted it said the image (without the head) of the Blessed Mother Mary is still there and remains a place of reverence. A crucifix has been erected and a small chapel to worship has been created inside the building.

Madonna Of The Windows

Looking at the window this Christmas Day,
You have come to me now in another way.
Oh, Lady of Fatima, why pick me?
Though known to me since I was three,
Mary, why do you speak to me today?
I wonder aloud as I start to pray,
Am I worthy to tell this wondrous tale?
What will the outcome be... and I pale.
Mary, how did this ever happen to me?
You know they rarely mentioned thee.
When I was taught about Jesus and God,
Why did they leave you lain beneath the sod?
"I'm not Catholic," protesting, I said.
"I'm Jewish," she replied. "Get that in your head.
Go on, brave heart, bare your soul today,
And on their knees, many more will pray.
For God is in you, is everywhere seen—
In the villages and cities, in the children's dream."
"O, Mary, Mary, afraid am I!"
"Hush now, my child, don't you cry,
For I will protect you. I'll pave the way.
All that's required is a prayer each day.
"Oh, Mary, Mary, what if they give me drugs?"
"They won't, my child. You'll receive many hugs."
"The last time your crucifixion, your Gethsemane.
"This time your heaven. . .for you are free."
Your guardian angels are standing true,
And an archangel is sent just for you.
Michael will lead you. Do not fret
As throughout the world this message is let.
Put it forth once again as before.
This time you're rocked in my arms evermore."

Chapter Three

MANIFESTING MY ANGEL

*I*n 1963, my first husband John and I miraculously survived a serious automobile accident. Following our recovery, John suggested we have another child. I was surprised but quickly consented, with one stipulation—that we have at least *two* more children. Our first three children, ages five, six, and seven, enjoyed a wonderful camaraderie and I did not want to raise a lonely "only" child, separated from older siblings by a significant age difference.

The timing was excellent. John's medical practice was thriving and Erick, Andy and Allison were in school full time. In 1964 we had a darling baby whom we named Michael. He was barely approaching his first birthday, and I was looking forward to having another baby. It was not to be, however, for a routine pap test revealed that I was in the early stages of cancer. The gynecologist recommended a hysterectomy, and in one fell swoop my hopes for a sister or brother for Michael were dashed. I was devastated.

After recovering from the surgery, however, John and I started talking about adopting a baby girl. I called agencies across the United States. Some told me to forget it because we already had four children. Some people laughed. Others suggested we seek a child from a foreign country. Yet, a strong, intuitive "knowingness" that my little girl was somewhere out there, just waiting for me, kept my resolve strong. I was especially sure of my quest when I prayed. Each evening before going to sleep I said the same prayer: *Thank you, God. I know my little girl is coming soon. Keep her safe.*

Each time I heard the same message from that small voice inside: *Have faith, she will come!*

After two years, however, those prayers had dwindled to about once a week. Then, one evening, I distinctly heard a woman's voice reply.

I hear you! she said with some exasperation, *It is done!*

The voice startled me, and when frightened, I often use humor to deflect the anxiety.

Is God a woman? I asked myself with a chuckle.

Suddenly, a clearly defined vision of Mother Mary, the mother of Jesus, appeared before my eyes. She wore the familiar blue garb: the colors were vivid; her countenance was lovely. She radiated love and looked just like the paintings I had studied in college in my art appreciation course. In the vision, Mary carried a baby wrapped in a pink blanket. As I watched in amazement, she reached out as if to hand the infant to me. Frightened, I sat upright in bed. The vision did not disappear.

Mary, I asked timidly, *is it really you?*

Yes, it is I, " she responded, *"Have patience. "*

The picture faded, leaving me astounded and very indignant. *Mary, you don't know what patience is!* I thought angrily, and was immediately ashamed of my preposterous and arrogant response. My momentary shame turned to elation.

A bit frightened but very excited, I woke up my husband to tell him of this extraordinary event. John's response was not quite what I had imagined; he was very upset and cautioned me not to tell anyone. He insisted that it was just a dream. But I knew it was *not* a dream. I *knew* that adoption was just around the corner. I *knew* a divine plan had been set into motion. I believed it with all my mind, heart and soul. My second daughter was coming!

But nothing happened. I called back all the agencies and my networking contacts. They offered no hope. Weeks grew into months, and my thoughts of adoption faded. Occasionally my eight-year-old daughter Allison would prompt pangs of longing when she asked, "Where is my little sister? I thought you said she was going to be born soon."

"Someday, darling," I replied. "When God wants us to have her, she will come."

Despite the delay, I truly believed that, and though raising four active youngsters kept me too busy to think about it during the day, there were many nights when I fell asleep thinking about Mother Mary handing me a baby. Sometimes, when the house had finally quieted, I would lie awake and think about the sudden appearance. *Why would Mother Mary come to me?* I wondered, then decided that Mary was the universal symbol of motherhood and passed it off as an association that my mind had made.

During this time, I was attending a small Methodist church. I briefly thought about talking to my minister about Mary's visits, then quickly abandoned that idea. These were definitely not ecumenical times. Mary was barely mentioned in our church liturgy, and more than one Protestant church organist had been reprimanded for playing *Ave Maria*.

In fact, I had wanted *Ave Maria* sung at my wedding, but my mother told me it could not be sung because it was a "Catholic hymn." I had reluctantly accepted that answer, but now, years later, I wondered what had prompted my request when I had never been taught to revere Mary. Perhaps my love of that aria also foretold of my future association with Mary.

The months turned into years. My days were busy caring for my children and studying at a nearby university. My goal was to combine my nursing education with a law degree. Once again, God had other plans.

One night my youngest sister Carly and her husband Vince came over for dinner and, on short notice, brought along two new friends. Carly and Vince were very special to me—I had introduced them on a blind date. Their friend, Kate, was lovely—tall, impeccably groomed and fashionable, with laughing green eyes and radiant auburn hair. Joe was handsome—tall and dark, with warm, dark-brown eyes. They were obviously in love, and as I would soon learn, they had an interesting history.

Kate had served as a nun for more than twenty-five years and Joe had been a parish priest. They had fallen in love and left their religious orders. They were now waiting for permission from Rome to be married.

As the evening progressed, the conversation turned to my adoption search.

"Oh, Barbara," Kate said excitedly, "I know a wonderful attorney who handles private adoptions."

She removed a small red address book from her smart, black leather purse and gave me his name and phone number. I took the card and casually put it in my pocket.

"I'll call him tomorrow. Thank you, Kate."

Shortly after our guests left, John and I headed to bed, both tired from the long week. We didn't discuss the information received from Kate; I just placed the paper with the attorney's contact information on my bedside table then slid between the sheets and fell soundly asleep. I was awakened abruptly at about 3:00 a.m. by a tugging at the sheet and the nightgown covering my arm. I turned on the lamp and looked around but saw nothing. When I turned it off I noticed a very bright, unusual light. It was a brilliant, incandescent gold color and it was quite literally *dancing* over the piece of paper!

I watched, fascinated, but for some reason, felt very scared. *Stay logical*, I told myself. *Look around for reflections. Was the light coming from the street light outside? No, it was not.* The light continued to dance as if having a life all its own. I lay still, not daring to breathe. Suddenly, the words of a little hymn I had learned as a child in Sunday school came to me, and I began to sing them very, very, softly:

> *Brighten the corner where you are.*
> *Brighten the corner where you are.*
> *Someone far from harbor*
> *You may guide across the bar.*
> *Brighten the corner where you are.*

The bright dancing light promptly disappeared. I took this as some sort of indication or divine sign that I should call the attorney. With that thought, a chill ran up my spine. I quickly decided not to mention this to John. His harsh words - *Just forget it! It must have been a dream!* - when I told him of Mary's first appearance still resounded in my head, and I had no desire for a repeat performance. Schooled in medicine, John was very uncomfortable with metaphysical experiences, and now any mention of Mary's name upset him.

Though I said nothing about the incident, I could think of little else the next morning as I bustled about the kitchen. I was standing by the sink when suddenly, in the middle of his breakfast, John started singing, "Brighten the corner where you are."

I audibly gasped and dropped a spoon in the sink. My husband seldom sang and certainly not while reading the newspaper and having his first cup of coffee! I knew from my psychology studies that because I had sung out loud, however softly, it increased his chances of doing this. But he was definitely not the singing type. And what an obscure song to sing. I took this as strong confirmation that I should follow up on the lead given to me by Kate.

I could hardly wait for John to leave for the hospital so I could make the call. As the phone rang, I reminded myself I was not into "magical" thinking and steeled myself against potential disappointment. The attorney was not in but his secretary took our address and said she would mail us an adoption application. When it arrived a few days later, I quickly completed it and headed for the mailbox. As I slipped it inside I said this small prayer:

God, please find my little girl.

Once again, I was hopeful, but the attorney never called. *Another false lead*, I thought, and finally surrendered. For more than *three years* my efforts had been in vain.

This is it, God! I give up! I will not try to adopt a child ever again, my thoughts screamed.

My children were all in school now. Michael, four years old, would attend morning preschool in the fall, and I would pursue my law degree full time. The lovely vision of the Madonna handing me a child now seemed like a faraway dream, and I found myself focused on the more distressing events of my physical reality.

It was 1968, turbulent times indeed. It was the summer following the assassinations of Senator Robert Kennedy and Dr. Martin Luther King. More than half a million American soldiers were fighting in Vietnam. Antiwar sentiments were running high. These events tore at my heart and soul. How does a young mother explain the shooting of our leaders to her children? Confused and afraid, my older children asked if we would be shot too. Nothing I said seemed to console them; nothing but my faith in God could prevail during these dark days.

One day Allison asked, "Do you think they shot our baby sister?"

I felt as if an arrow had entered my heart.

"No," I replied calmly, "I know she is safe, wherever she is."

My disappointment, the assassinations, the war, the killings, caused me to question whether I believed in God and even whether God existed. I began to doubt everything I had been taught in church. Once, while taking my nightly walk, I cried openly for being a fool and letting my imagination run away with me.

Where is my little girl, Mary? I trusted you to bring me my baby.

That August, the children and I left for the New England coast, where we owned a small cottage. We all loved the beach, and these magical weeks were a tradition that we looked forward to all year.

Joining us on vacation was the children's favorite baby-sitter, Crissi. This mature, sunny sixteen-year-old had been with us for four years, and her assistance gave me time to rest, to read, take long strolls on the beach and forget the pain of world events. I would often go for solitary walks in the evening. The sounds of the water and the sight of the far-flung stars eased my aching soul and made me feel at one with God again. This year, I also hoped that during the quiet times I would find peace with the little girl I would never know. The seed that Mary had planted still resided deep within my soul. Still, I tried to ignore the hurt and release the hope that I would find my little daughter.

The first evening of vacation I sat alone at the water's edge, hugging my knees and rocking. Under the stars, watching the light dance over the dark ocean waters, I felt very close to God. Thoughts of the little baby girl crept into my mind once again. Why couldn't I just forget her? Suddenly I felt angry at my innocence in having believed that Mary appeared to me or that she was the divine contact

34

between my baby girl and me. Hadn't she sent an ex-nun to give me the person's name who would find me the child?

"Oh," I moaned, "what a *stupid* little fool I have been!" I then turned my anguish on who I believed to be the real culprit. *God, why don't you leave me alone? Why won't these thoughts go away?*

The answer came from the still, small voice within. *Have patience. We are testing your resolve.*

"I don't want my resolve tested, okay?" I shouted. "Forget it! I'm done! I don't believe in anything anymore. I need to be shown!"

Looking out over the horizon, I was astonished to once again see the outline of a motherly figure, holding a babe in her arms.

"Oh, no!" I began to cry in frustration.

Shaking my head in disbelief, I looked again. The vision came into sharp focus. It was the Madonna. She was dressed in her traditional blue robe. In her arms she cradled a baby.

"Are you real?" I asked.

She did not answer.

Her serious countenance changed now to a sweet smile. Gazing down at the baby, she kissed it on the forehead, then reached out as if offering it to me. Then the image disappeared and my eyes filled with tears. I felt deeply disturbed and frightened that something must be wrong with my mind. I could not tell my husband, as he often joked derisively about "my visions."

Please God, I beseeched through my tears, *help me!*

I quickly left the beach and went back into the house where I climbed into bed under a fuzzy summer blanket. I could tell no one about the episode.

Have faith. That was the thought passing unbidden through my mind. "Be quiet. Please leave me alone," I moaned and eventually cried myself to sleep.

In the morning I awakened refreshed, as if the tears had cleansed my memories. I took my older youngsters, now eight, nine and ten, to the beach. Crissi stayed behind with four-year-old Michael, who was more interested in playing with his toys than in flying kites at the beach on this cool, windy August day.

I sat watching the children launch and fly their colorful box kites. I felt so thankful as I looked at their strong, tanned bodies.

Thank you, God, for my children, I prayed quickly. *How selfish of me to want another child.* When I said those words, I experienced a strange tug in my chest. Even now, I find it hard to describe the sensation, except to say it felt as if a butterfly were flying out of my heart.

At that precise moment I heard Crissi calling me. I turned and saw her running toward me, half dragging Michael behind her.

"Phone! Phone! Mrs. B., come quick!" She was screaming and laughing in excitement. "Someone's on the phone who says your baby daughter has been born!"

"What?" I screamed. My heart was beating fast.

"A baby! A baby!" Crissi kept yelling, and Michael was

jumping up and down in excitement.

My thoughts were racing. What? Who? How?

I ran to the house. By the time I answered the phone, I was breathless and my voice and hands were shaking.

"Hello, Barbara! This is Tom McKenna, the attorney from Florida. Your daughter was born just about two hours ago. I know it's been some time since you heard from me, but we've had a run of boys born."

"Some time!" I said loudly. "Some time!" I repeated incredulously. "It's been *two years!*"

"Do you still want to adopt a baby?" he asked calmly.

My emotions were on a roller coaster. The tears were flowing, and the sobs sought to escape. I composed myself and answered evenly,

"Well, I'm going to have to talk with my husband. He won't be here until the weekend."

"Oh no, you better call me back by tomorrow morning at nine," he warned. "I've a long waiting list."

"All right," I said.

I probably can call you back in ten minutes if I can connect with John, I thought.

I immediately called his office. "Sorry, he's not here. He's delivering a baby," his nurse said efficiently.

"Have him call me as soon as possible."

"Is something wrong?"

"Oh, no, just some family stuff."

Within thirty minutes the phone rang. Quickly I informed my husband of the news, all the while reminding myself not to mention Mary.

John didn't hesitate; he knew how important this was to me. "I'll fly to Florida to pick her up this weekend, if that's okay with them. Find out if you need to be there."

"Oh, but I want to go!" I responded.

My husband then devised a very practical plan so as not to disturb the children's vacation, saying if we did they would resent their new baby sister. I acquiesced, then we hung up so I could call the attorney back. I was ready to dial when a small intuitive voice advised, *Stop, wait!*

Contrary to my impulsive nature, I decided to sleep on it and call the attorney in the morning.

That evening, Crissi and I could barely contain our excitement. Our broad smiles and giggles were quickly picked up by my oldest son, Erick.

"What are you and Crissi laughing about, Mom?" he asked.

"Oh, girl stuff," I replied casually.

"I think you have a secret," he persisted.

"We do," I admitted, "and I will tell you about it in a few days."

Erick agreed not to say anything to the others about the secret, but shortly thereafter, Allison and Andy came bounding into the living room.

"Mommy, Mommy, tell us the secret," Andy cried out.

"In a few days," I answered. "Why don't you and Crissi go out for ice cream?"

"Yay! Yay!" they shouted in response, and moments later they were racing out the door.

I was alone at last and had time to gather my thoughts. I was still reeling from the news. A baby! Another daughter! Already born.

"Oh, Mary! How could I have doubted you? I am so grateful." My thoughts raced as I thought of a newborn's needs. But something was wrong. My intuitive nature was sending me a very unsettled feeling. In fact, I was uneasy at my core. I decided to go for a walk on the beach and pray about it. I walked for a mile or so before finally returning to the house. The uneasiness persisted.

At eleven o'clock, the household was silent, and I called my husband.

"Something isn't right," I told him. "I'm not feeling good about this baby. In fact, the thought of adopting her is nauseating me."

"What?" he shouted, his frustration clearly coming through now. "You've waited years for this day!"

"I know, but something's wrong," I added lamely. "I don't know how to explain it."

We quickly said our good-byes.

"I'll call you tomorrow," I said sadly and replaced the phone on the cradle.

What is the matter? I asked myself. Then the answer came. I just did not feel that this child was my daughter.

You're a fool, my rational side told me.

Near midnight, I went out to the water's edge and placed my feet in the cool salt water. All the beachfront homes were darkened. The sky was a deep midnight blue and the stars sparkled brighter than I had ever remembered. The only sound was the surf lapping on the shore. I was alone with my thoughts.

I sat down on the cool, hard sand and hugged my legs as the emotions of the day caught up with me. Placing my head down on my knees, I gently cried, "What is the matter?"

I knew my discomfort had nothing to do with my plans to attend law school. I would have given up a law degree in a heartbeat to adopt my baby girl, so why every time I thought about doing so did I feel sick?

Please, God, I prayed. *Please tell me what to do.*

As I gazed out at the horizon a clear vision of the head of the Blessed Mother Mary appeared clearly before me once again. She was draped in a dazzling white headpiece, and the stars seemed to dance around her head in a circle.

Your daughter is yet to be born, she said firmly and distinctly.

What? I cried out to her in pure frustration. But she had already faded from view.

I do not pretend to understand how or why these appearances of Mary occurred, but my heart told me immediately that the message was correct. A peace passed over me as if an angel had caressed every cell in my body.

This was the "peace that passeth understanding," I decided. This was divine intervention, and I was *not* going to adopt this child. As soon as I reached that resolution a sense of harmony pervaded my soul.

I left the beach for the house, still weeping silently for the child who would not be known to me, yet mindful of the other woman who would experience the immeasurable joy of being her mother. I also then became aware that there was another mother, the biological one, undergoing severe pain at the loss of her child. I prayed for her also.

"Okay," John said, resigned and rather fed up, when I called him with my decision. "You have to raise her." At the time, I did not know how prophetic that statement would be.

A profound sense of relief, followed by intense sadness, occurred as I placed the call to the attorney.

"Congratulations, Mommy," McKenna's secretary said sweetly when I identified myself.

My heart plummeting, I did not respond. She then put me through to the attorney, who was exasperated with my explanation that I sensed something wrong with adopting that particular baby.

"Nothing's wrong," he said, "A pediatrician and a neurologist have examined the baby. She is perfect!"

My heart leaped, but I remained steadfast. I would definitely follow Mother Mary's directive.

He paused for a moment, then added. "We do have another woman in labor. If she has a little girl, do you want us to call you?"

At that moment an electrical shock ran through my body.

It was so strong that I was physically knocked about a foot from the spot where I was standing. My heart beat wildly. Suddenly a vision of Mother Mary appeared in the kitchen!

This is your daughter! she said, and instantly faded away.

This time, her appearance did not frighten me, and though I didn't dare tell anyone, every cell in my body believed the truth of her words. The baby about to be born was indeed *my* baby, the soul who had chosen our family to support her during her lessons here on earth.

"Yes," I said to McKenna, "yes, yes, that is my baby. *I know it!*"

"Don't get your hopes up. A lot of baby boys have been born here lately," he said grimly.

I *knew* this was a little baby girl, just as I had known the gender of my other children and had picked out their names before they were born.

I could hardly endure the wait. Time was dragging. I made the beds, did the dishes, dusted, vacuumed the house, did laundry. I did anything to stay busy. My mounting excitement did not allow me to read, so I tried to work a jigsaw puzzle, then a crossword puzzle, to no avail. I could not leave the telephone, so I paced back and forth from the living room to the family room. I was a smoker back then, and that day I chain-smoked, lighting one cigarette with the butt of another. My abdomen and lower back were hurting, as if I was in labor. I suddenly realized that in all the excitement I hadn't told John what was going on. I placed the call.

"Whatever you say," he said with disgust in his tone, then quickly hung up the phone.

Finally, the phone rang. My heart raced.

"Barbara, you have a beautiful healthy baby girl." McKenna's enthusiasm was clear as he added, "She is just perfect, a gorgeous child."

"This is wonderful! Oh, so wonderful," I repeated, crying. "Oh, thank you, dear Mary, thank you. Please have her examined by a pediatrician."

"Of course," he said. "If we find any problems, I'll call you back right away."

"Okay, but no matter what, she is my daughter," I said vehemently. Even if something was physically or mentally wrong, it didn't matter. I was certain that I would adopt this child.

John made the flight arrangements. Because he was a physician, he was allowed to fly south to bring her home without my accompanying him. I still ached to go and hold my daughter in my arms but John's pragmatism prevailed. The children were told that "our secret" was that they were going to have a little sister, Amy. They were all very excited and ran out to tell their friends.

I then called my sister, Carly, who was expecting her third child, to give her the news and thank her for bringing Kate and Joe to dinner. I never saw Kate or Joe again after that night, and I believe Kate was Mother Mary's messenger and Carly and her husband Vince were the catalysts.

Soon my phone rang incessantly as news of the impending adoption spread over the beach. The next afternoon when I arrived at the beach front, the neighbors yelled, "Surprise!"

Pink crepe-paper streamers hung from brightly-colored beach chairs and umbrellas along the waterfront. Gift boxes wrapped in shiny pink paper were piled high on a beach blanket, awaiting my arrival. This child seemed to be everyone's baby, and the women of the beachfront community spent the next four days until Amy's arrival chattering and laughing in anticipation. I could hardly contain my excitement, and sleep was nearly impossible.

I spent my next few nights by the water, communing with the stars and hoping for a glimpse of the vision of Mary. I so desperately wanted to thank her. I prayed for her to make an appearance to no avail. I was disappointed. Where was Mother Mary? Why would she not appear? I did not know.

My heart overflowed with joy, but I was also acutely aware that my joy was another woman's sorrow. I prayed for this mother many, many times, even though I did not know her circumstances.

John called from the Boston airport. "She's a little doll and a good little girl," he said hurriedly. "She took one bottle on the plane and is still sleeping."

"Oh, I can't wait to hold her," I said joyfully.

"I'll be there soon."

* * *

"She's here!" Andy called out, a broad grin splitting his face. He was a fairly quiet child, so his shout startled me. We all ran outside and spotted John's dark green car coming up the road. My excitement mounted, and I started to weep with joy as my husband climbed out of the car and reached back into a white wicker bassinet. I came forward, and he placed a beautiful baby girl in my arms. She was all wrapped up in a new pink summer blanket.

"Hello, little Amy," I said, cuddling her to my breast.

"Welcome to the world! We have waited a long, long time for you. I love you!"

Her perfectly shaped round head was framed by silky dark hair forming ringlets around her face. Her cheeks were incredible! They were high, prominent and perfectly formed. She was a most beautiful baby. The exquisite turquoise eyes that she still has today opened wide and met mine in an even gaze.

It was then that a chill traveled down my spine, and the hair on my arms stood up. This was a connection felt deeply at the soul level. *I've known her before. Perhaps in another lifetime.* I had never had that kind of thought before that moment.

Suddenly a lightbulb went on in my head. Today is the fourteenth of the month! That means that Amy was born on the ninth of August! Erick was born on the ninth, as was Allison. Andy and Michael's birthdays, the fourth and fifth, added up to nine. *Was this significant?* I wondered. What made me think of that then? I had never noticed numbers before, never heard of numerology. But I knew now that this was more than just a coincidence—this was synchronicity.

"Let me hold her! She's my baby," said eight-year-old Allison, who stood impatiently by my side in her yellow-and-orange flowered bikini. Placing her in Allison's arms for the first time, I thought, *my little girls are reunited at last.* That evening I rocked our little Amy and sang the same lullaby I had sung to all my children:

Mommy's little baby,

Mommy's little girl.

I love Mommy's baby,

Mommy loves her girl.

After placing Amy in her bassinet and retiring for the night, I instantly fell sound asleep, only to be suddenly awakened with a shake. There was the vision of Mother Mary once again. This time she appeared dressed in a brilliant white robe. She held forth empty outstretched arms, as if in a blessing. She was smiling sweetly, and as she faded from sight I thought I heard a baby crying. I shook myself awake. This was no dream. It was time to get up for a three o'clock feeding. The circle was complete.

This thought was sent to me as I sat there feeding my daughter:

"An adopted baby grows in its mother's heart."

***

Sadly, John and I would divorce; he died in 1995.

My second husband, Chip, would formally adopt Amy at age eight and raise her as his own daughter. She married at age twenty-one, only to lose her beloved husband in an industrial explosion just months after their wedding. Amy, a beautiful young woman, has not remarried. She is now 50 years old and living in the Northeast, near her sister Allison.

The Littlest Angel

Sitting by the sea one day,
She visits me now in another way.
I see the vision, I hear the voice,
This time there is a different choice.
A babe held in your arms so strong,
Is this the child for whom I long?
"Will she come to me yet another day?"
I lovingly ask as I continue to pray.
And then my faith brought you home,
A seed that God had surely sown.
"Where did you come from, baby dear?"
"Out of the nowhere, into the here."
Spirit has surely sent you this day!
Holding her close, I continue to pray.
Bright blue eyes gazing at me
Looking more and more like Thee.
"I came to join my family,
I bring you love through divinity.
Sent to you from the highest source,
From Infinite Mind, the strongest force.
"You thought me into reality."
My heart cries out, "Can this be?"
And clutching you to my breast as before.
My daughter you'll be forever more.

Chapter Four

MOTHER MARY MANIFESTS AGAIN

"When I find myself in times of trouble,
Mother Mary comes to me."

~John Lennon

*M*om! MOM! HURRY! Something's wrong with Allie!" The sound of Michael's boots crashing down the stairs was the only warning I had of my daughter's crisis. I quickly left my comfortable chair and bolted up the stairs and into Allison's room.

Allison was standing, bent over, next to her bed. Her small, delicate hands were placed protectively on her melon-sized abdomen.

"Don't be upset, Mom," she said calmly, "I'm in labor. I was raped."

Her words seared my soul.

"Who?" I demanded. "When?"

"It's not important now," she said wisely.

I had been with my nineteen-year-old daughter, Allison, almost daily for the last nine months and had no idea she was pregnant. With each question dozens of possible answers raced chaotically through my mind. Suddenly my vision blurred, my legs weakened, and my knees buckled. I was reeling, in danger of losing consciousness. *God, give me strength,* I prayed fervently.

A thought immediately entered my mind in response: *Your strength cometh from the Lord who made heaven and earth.*

Instantly, my body strengthened, and my heart and soul were filled with peace at the deepest level, enabling my training as a registered nurse to take over.

"Have you had prenatal care?"

"No."

"Okay," I said, and sorted through what needed immediate attention.

"Lie down so I can time your contractions."

The situation seemed surrealistic, as if I were split into thirds. One part of me performed professionally and unemotionally as a nurse. Another part, the first-time, excited grandmother, was also in evidence. Allison was my eldest daughter and my first biological grandchild was about to make an appearance on this earth.

Meanwhile, the third of me that was Allison's mother was in agony. My little girl, raped? She had carried this pain alone for nine long months . . . going to work each day . . . listening to my admonitions because she had allowed her slim, athletic body to become plump. My heart became heavy with the exquisite ache I believe is reserved for mothers.

Suddenly a vivid picture of Mother Mary came into my mind. I could see her face clearly as she beckoned to me. She was standing, robed in white, suspended in a gleaming golden light as she pointed to a babe cradled in her right arm. I shook my head in disbelief—she appeared to be standing right next to me.

I will be with you, her countenance seemed to say.

Amazed and a bit shaken to see her once again, I began to weep. *Oh, Mary, thank you for coming to me again after all these years,* I cried, as I sank to my knees in reverence and grief.

I had received a beautiful gift from God with the adoption of Amy. Would I now have to give up my first grandchild to another family? Was this the law of cause and effect?

NO! NO! I screamed silently. *I cannot do that.*

Although Mary's appearance startled me at first, she was now providing comfort, letting me know that all would go well. It was then that my pain and the sense of it became obvious. This is what Amy's biological mother had felt, and this is what Mary must have felt as a mother—the sorrow of losing a child.

I rapidly dismissed that thought, because I knew I was experiencing only a fraction of the pain suffered by the Virgin Mother Mary while witnessing her son's crucifixion. I focused on Mother Mary's greater loss and pain and used it for my own solace.

Mary, I prayed, *I am so sorry that you had to watch your son die. What agony you must have felt. How did you bear the pain? Oh, how my heart hurts for you! I know if you got through that, I can get through this. But I need your help.*

Please be with me now.

As I finished my quick prayer, the glowing vision of Mary faded, but my emotional strength and courage returned.

Allison's contractions, growing stronger and lasting longer, demanded my full attention. I needed to find an obstetrician fast. I picked up her phone and called one of the nearby hospitals.

"You're lucky to get him on this weekend," the operator said after giving me the name of the obstetrician on call. "He's the best!"

My work history in hospitals had taught me that the operators knew everything about the medical staff. I was bolstered by the good news, but only momentarily. As I returned the princess phone to its cradle I thought, *my little girl is not a princess anymore.* The pink phone now seemed incongruous with the unfolding events.

I called the doctor and, feeling utterly foolish, related the facts. He was very understanding and we agreed to meet in the emergency room.

I hung up the phone and walked down the stairs as if in a trance, the cozy family scene before me a sharp contrast with what I was about to tell them.

"Chip," I said as calmly as possible, "Allison is in labor and we have to go to the hospital."

"What?" he shouted and jumped to his feet. "It can't be—she's not pregnant," he added indignantly.

"Yes, she is and we have to go," I said firmly.

Not trusting my husband or myself to drive our precious

cargo, and knowing that Allison would need professional assistance should a rapid delivery ensue, I phoned 911 for an ambulance. My thoughts were solely of Allison and how alone she must have felt while carrying her secret for nine months. I was also concerned about her labor because I had experienced a difficult first birth.

While Allison and I sat on her lovely, white, quilted bedspread and waited for the ambulance to arrive, I wrapped my arms around her and crooned the lullaby I had sung to her many years before.

Mommy's little baby

Mommy's little girl

I love Mommy's baby

Mommy loves her girl

Inane words, but the pretty tune always seemed to soothe her.

"Don't be afraid, Allie," I said with false bravado. I was shaking inside.

Soon the red revolving lights of the ambulance shone through her white bedroom draperies and swept an eerie shadow across the walls and ceiling.

"I will always be here for you, honey," I said.

On the way to the hospital my husband and I discussed our adopting this grandchild. We did not have time to make the decision. As soon as we arrived at the hospital, events happened quickly, including a series of mystical coincidences. These coincidences would, in my opinion, convince even the most steadfast skeptic of the presence of a higher power in the universe—one I call God.

The admitting clerk was a professional young woman wearing a tailored navy-blue pinstripe suit. She was very empathetic to our plight.

"Oh, how can this be? How could I not have known?" I repeated over and over as tears welled up in my eyes. I had often heard of young women carrying their babies to term without their parents knowing they were pregnant. As a nurse I never understood how that could be possible. Now I had firsthand experience. Feelings of guilt and failure swept over me as we answered the questions on the admissions form.

Having finished her interview, the young admissions officer leaned across her desk and took my hand. "Everything will be fine," she said with confidence. "You and God are a majority. This is my first night on duty as a hospital-administration intern, I will personally watch over Allison and pray for perfect adoptive parents for the baby."

"Thank you…" I floundered for her name.

"My name is Sister Miriam."

My eyes widened. This was the seventies, but where I came from nuns didn't wear crisp white blouses with business suits, leather pumps, and sheer nylons. And so the magic of synchronicity began to be revealed. My prayer to Mary had already been answered by Sister Miriam's presence. Just as with Amy's adoption, a nun was to play a primary role in the adoption of my grandchild. I almost told her about Amy's adoption and Mother Mary's appearances, but decided this was not the time.

In my heart I knew that, from the many possible choices, Mary had directed me to this particular hospital. Convinced that my prayer was answered, my demeanor became calm and sure. I accepted that I was entering a painful period of growth for my soul.

Allison was in labor all night. I stayed with her while my husband dozed fitfully in the waiting room. She and I talked softly. Her long, straight, wheat-colored hair was now very wet from the exertion of labor. As I lovingly stroked her brow and rubbed her back she, at last, confided in me as to what had happened to her.

While Allison was at a neighborhood party, one of the young men she knew had asked her to come into a bedroom to talk with him. She went, feeling perfectly safe. The idea of being raped in this upper-class neighborhood never entered her mind. These parties were held in very large homes and the average attendance was nearly one hundred people. With the noise of the conversation and the rock music blaring, Allison's calls for help went unnoticed.

"Why didn't you tell me, sweetheart?" I asked.

"After I discovered that I was pregnant, I decided I didn't want you to hurt for all those months, Mom," she explained, her almond eyes brimming with tears. "Besides, I made an appointment to have an abortion."

That stunned me, but before I had a chance to react she related the following story to me.

Her abortion had been scheduled for a Saturday morning on a crisp fall day. On Friday, Allison was waiting for the elevator in the building where she worked. The elevator cage zoomed up past her floor, then stopped, and came back down. When the doors parted *no one was inside*. But what looked like a MasterCard—orange, black, and white—was on the floor, leaning against the back wall.

"I thought someone had dropped a credit card so I picked it up and looked for the cardholder's name. But it was a facsimile of a MasterCard, and it read 'Put Christ in Charge of Your Life.'

"Finding this card was earthshaking to me. How had it gotten there? Why at that moment?" she added, pensively.

I understood her confusion. Allison had always been very alert, very perceptive and most of all, logical. As a child I took her to Sunday school and church every week, but as a teenager, she rebelled against church. I respected her right to explore other or even no religious beliefs and institutions. After she had sifted through the evidence of the existence of a higher power, examined the circumstances surrounding Jesus' birth, and asked questions about the millions of non-Christians in the world, Allison proclaimed herself an agnostic.

"I stuck the card in my pocket and planned to go through with the abortion scheduled for the next morning."

"But the card persuaded you otherwise?" I asked.

Now another wave of contractions gripped her, and I watched the heartrate and blood-pressure displays on the bedside monitor. The readout showed that she and the baby were doing fine. When the contractions subsided, she continued with her story.

"Yes, the card and another incident," she answered. "Do you remember when we were having a cup of tea at the breakfast table and Amy got all upset 'cause of a nightmare?"

I nodded. How could I have forgotten? Amy had screamed, then ran downstairs and flew into my arms.

"Mommy! Mommy!" she wailed. "I had a terrible nightmare!"

"What was it about, honey?" I asked, holding her tightly on my lap and kissing the top of her head.

"I dreamed someone flushed me down the toilet!" she cried. "Oh, it was so terrible."

As I thought back on this incident, I realized how devastating Amy's outburst would have been for Allison—considering Amy's adoption at five days of age.

"My heart nearly stopped and dropped out onto the floor," Allison admitted. "I was about to do to my baby what Amy had dreamed about. I was going to have an abortion. I was going to flush my child down the drain, down the toilet."

A shudder ran through her as she remembered how she had felt.

"I decided at that moment I couldn't have an abortion. Someone or something—a power greater than I—was involved in the events and influencing them. I decided to cancel the abortion and trust this higher authority..." She laughed nervously. "But, Mom, I was so scared!"

So months earlier, as she looked at her beloved little sister, with her long chestnut hair and bright turquoise eyes, Allison knew in the depth of her being that she was meant to give birth and give the baby up for adoption.

"I know you and Chip want to adopt this baby..." She

hesitated, always the diplomat, choosing the right words. "But you have too many children now, and I think my baby should go to younger parents."

My mind knew she was right, but my heart was breaking. I loved children. How could I ever give up this baby? This was, after all, my first grandchild. But Allison's story and her decision resonated deeply within me, at the soul level. I became resolved to follow her wishes. I decided then not to go with her into the delivery room. I realized that if I saw her son—somehow, I was certain that she was having a boy—I could never let him go.

I stayed with Allison until about eight in the morning, when she was moved to the delivery room. The obstetrical nurses had promised me that they would call me when the baby was born. As I watched her being wheeled away, my heart was filled with anguish.

Why is this happening? I wondered. *Is this my test—to give up my own first grandchild to strangers?*

My very essence screamed, *No!*

Exhausted, I went to join my husband in the waiting room. I clung to him as sobs wracked my body. But then I remembered Mother Mary and what she had endured. This thought again gave me a sense of calmness and peace pervaded my soul and a feeling of courage returned.

The ride home, though just a half hour, seemed endless. The telephone rang within ten minutes of our entering the door.

"A healthy baby boy," the nurse reported. "He's just perfect and weighs a little over eight pounds. Allison is doing just fine."

Deprived of sleep and in deep emotional pain, I was infuriated by the nurse's cheerful demeanor.

Fine? Fine? I screamed silently. *No, she is not fine, and neither am I.*

My inner voice sobbed, and the anger rose in my throat as I thought, *I will never see this child, never rock him, never gaze at his face, nor see his eyes widen at the wonder of the newly fallen snow. NO! Everything is not fine!*

I continued to sob deeply as I trudged upstairs, washed my face, and reached for my favorite light flannel nightgown. Usually this gown had a comforting effect, but I couldn't sleep. Finally, I got dressed and went to the real estate office where I worked as a relocation counselor—a position I enjoyed because it was a "caring profession." It gave me a flexibility nursing did not, allowing me to attend to the demands of my home and children. The broker's wife, Sharon, had become a dear and understanding friend.

Getting out of my car in the parking lot, I slowly made my way to my office door. My legs felt like lead. I did not feel like being there that day but did not know where else to go. I could not stay home. I could not look at Allison's bedroom.

Please, Mother Mary, stay by my side, I begged, tears filling my eyes. Oh, how I had longed for this day when I would become a first-time grandmother.

"And now I will not even be able to hold him!" I exclaimed, then, shaking my fist at the stand of stately trees now full with the blossoms of spring, I began to cry once again.

As I approached the steps to the back entrance to our office a shiny object, almost concealed in the grass, caught my eye. The early morning sunlight reflected a gleaming white light.

"Oh," I thought in amazement. "I haven't seen that bright a light since I last saw Mother Mary at Amy's adoption."

I bent down and picked up the object. It was a sterling silver, religious medal bearing a picture of the Virgin Mary. My whole body shivered in recognition of this huge moment in my life. My legs became weak. I was now convinced that Mary was with me, guiding me. Allison must be fulfilling a divine purpose. Overcome with humility and awe, I sank to my knees there on the grass and prayed.

Oh, God, Mother Mary, I beseeched. *What is happening?* I then thought, foolishly, that I didn't know any Catholic prayers, so I said what was in my heart. *Thank you, thank you, for being with me in my hour of need.*

And now I could see Mother Mary clearly standing before me, again suspended in an incredible golden light. Her outstretched arms and her very presence comforted me. Her countenance full of love calmed me. She did not speak but her arms seemed to encircle me. My heart and soul were filled with a profound peace. I once again experienced the "peace that passeth understanding."

I sensed that I had stumbled on a great secret of universal law. Mary, Jesus, God, angels—they were all with me, always available to me to call on them. I now felt certain that everything about this miraculous birth had been planned and would turn out perfectly. I just did not know how or why. Even Allison's rape had a spiritual purpose. I just did not know what it was. At that moment I let go of the outcome.

With the medal of Mary clutched in my hand, I shakily ascended the stairs and entered the quiet, deserted office. I called the hospital to see how Allison was doing.

"I'm okay, Mom," she responded softly. "I named the baby Christopher, for Christ, because of the card I found in the elevator."

Her young voice sounded so solemn, sadness overwhelmed me once again. Yet at the same time my heart leaped at her decision, which I knew was another part of the miracle's unfolding. I quickly reached for the medal of Mary that I now carried in my pocket, put it to my lips and kissed it for strength.

"That is a wonderful choice, sweetheart," I replied, "I'll call our attorney and find out how to proceed with the adoption if that's what you want."

I was bravely saying all the right words, but my voice sounded far away, as if I were on automatic pilot.

"Okay, Mom," Allie replied. "Remember, God and you are a majority. Everything will be okay."

Oh, poor Christopher Robin, I thought after we hung up. I don't know what made me think of that poem at the moment. I sat looking through the office windows toward the building across the street, where our attorney rented his professional suite. *Poor Christopher Robin. Poor Christopher Robin.*

Those words replayed themselves as I lay my head on my desk. Thoroughly exhausted, physically, mentally, emotionally, and spiritually, I dropped off to sleep.

"Barbara? Barbara, are you all right?" A soft hand touched my shoulder. It was my dear friend Sharon.

"What?" she gasped in disbelief when I told her what had happened, "I saw Allison two days ago. She wasn't pregnant!"

"Yes, she was."

I then tearfully explained Allison's decision to give baby Christopher up for adoption. I also told her that we would not charge for the adoption; we would be happy if someone would just pay Allison's one-day hospital costs and the attorney's fees.

Sharon looked at me with widening eyes.

"Oh, Barbara," she said, her tone both excited and tender, "I have a wonderful friend in California who wants to adopt a baby but can't because the cost is astronomical. Please let me call her."

I wanted to know everything about the couple. Sharon told me that the woman and her husband had a wonderful marriage but could not have children of their own due to a traumatic accident. She was an artist and had been valedictorian of her class. She and Sharon, both about ten years older than Allison, had been college pals.

"They are a gifted, creative couple," she said, her excitement growing, "And they would make fabulous parents! Her husband's a great guy!"

"What does he do?" I asked.

"Carpentry, but he's going to apply to chiropractic or medical school, I think."

Oh, great! I thought, *a carpenter, just like Jesus.* My imagination was really running away with me.

Trusting and respecting Sharon's impeccable opinion of people, I gave her permission to contact her friend. She hurried into her office and placed the call while I put my head down on my desk and dozed again. Clutched in my hand was the religious medal of Mary. In the background, I heard faint bits of the conversation: ". . . upper middle-class family . . . very attractive . . . athletic . . . smart . . . "

Even now, it seems like a dream.

"Barbara, can you arrange for a neurologist and a pediatrician to see the baby?" Sharon was back at my desk, beaming down at me. "Laura is so excited! She and her husband wish to adopt the baby, pending the doctors' examinations."

"Laura?" I asked.

"Yes, my friend."

"Laura" was the title of the song that my now-deceased father had always asked me to play on the organ when he came to visit. Was this another mystical coincidence, or was I going off the deep end?

No, I decided. *This means that Christopher is going to his rightful new home.*

Sister Miriam had prayed with us for perfect parents. Although I knew this adoption decision was spiritually aligned with God's purpose, my tears flowed once again.

"Let me call our attorney," I said, and just like that the adoption of little Christopher was set into motion.

Laura and Allen flew in from California to meet with our attorney. Sharon kept me informed of the progress of the adoption.

"They're changing his name," she told me. "They're calling him Richard."

Chills and shivers traveled the length of my spine and my hair stood up on both arms. Richard was my twin brother's name.

A few long days later I was sitting in our office with a corporate client. My desk overlooked the parking lot and street. I watched as an attractive young couple got out of their car. The young woman had long, straight, strawberry-blonde hair, and the handsome young man was bearded. She carried a baby wrapped in a blanket.

"Look," my client remarked, "Don't they look like a modern-day nativity scene?"

As soon as the words left his mouth, I realized that I was watching my grandson and his new parents going to the nearby attorney's office to finalize the adoption papers.

I quickly excused myself and went into the bathroom. I clutched the sink for support as my knees began to buckle and I slowly sank to the floor. I could not stand; my grief was too much to bear. The tears now became sobs, and I heard excerpts from Handel's *Messiah* as I sat on the floor of the tiny bathroom.

"Surely, surely He has borne our grief and carried our sorrows."

The music did not console me; I did not even question the fact that I was hearing it. I just hoped my client could not hear me sobbing. I tried to stand, but once more collapsed in anguish. Then Mother Mary again appeared to me in a golden light. This time Mary put her arms around me, pulled me to her bosom and rocked me.

It will all be fine, she promised. Christopher *is with his rightful parents now,"* she said softly and gently, *"We have been arranging this for some time. You must believe that Allison was the channel that carried the soul to his parents. All is as planned."*

And then she was gone once again. Slowly rising from the floor, I felt a sense of strength and composure. Phrases from my favorite book *The Prophet* by Kahlil Gibran, began to bounce around in my thoughts, consoling me.

"Your children are not your children."

"They belong not to you."

"They come through you but not from you. . ."

"You may house their body but not their souls. . ."

"You are the bows from which your children as living arrows are sent forth."

"They belong to the Universe."

It was then I surrendered and accepted Christopher's adoption to be of a divine nature.

* * *

If that were the end of this story, it could be considered a wondrous tale of miracles and synchronicity. But there is more. Our lives in a small New England town provided only one-half of the equation.

The other half of the story, as told to me by Sharon, had unfolded across the continent. In California, before we even knew of them, Laura and Allen co-led a church group with another couple who were expecting a baby at any moment. Laura's sister and brother-in-law also had recently adopted a baby—a very expensive proposition. Surrounded by people who were having children, and knowing the cost of adoption, Laura and Allen were feeling hopeless about ever having a child. Then Allen had a dream. In it, a tall, bearded man in a long white robe stood holding a lamb in the crook of one arm. His other hand grasped a staff. "Allen, Allen" the man called, "you are going to have a son, and you will name him Richard."

Allen described this dream to his wife the next day. He felt deeply troubled because the dream had been so real. Although he had never had a vision, he was certain that this was indeed a materialization. Shaken, he called his minister for counseling and guidance. The men concluded that the dream had been the result of the stress Allen was feeling because his friends and relatives were having babies and because of his intense longing for a child.

Early the next morning Laura received the phone call from Sharon about Christopher's birth. In compliance with Allen's dream, they renamed their miracle baby Richard.

* * *

And still there is more. When my husband Chip and I were married, we found a perfect home to accommodate our family. Unfortunately, because of its location, Allison, then seventeen, was forced to transfer to a new high school for her senior year. She accepted the situation and, making the best of it, became determined to win the position of starting right wing on the girls' hockey team. This was an ambitious goal because her new school held the state championship and had a very strong team.

On the day Allison and I went to the high school to register her, we walked past a beautifully painted athletic mural that included a young girl playing hockey. The girl held a hockey stick in her hand, and her long, straight, golden hair lifted from her shoulders as she ran toward the goal.

"Hey, Allie, here you are," I said, somewhat startled, because the resemblance to my daughter was uncanny.

She stopped and stared at the mural. "Boy, Mom, it really does look like me," she agreed, laughing lightly.

We learned later from Sharon that the mural artist is Christopher's adoptive mother, Laura, who graduated from that very same high school many years before.

Mary, I thought, *you are perfect.*

Allie went on to become the starting forward on the hockey team. Her team captured the state championship once again.

Not surprisingly, I think often of those hours and days that profoundly influenced me. The circumstances surrounding Christopher's birth and adoption gave both Allison and me a gift of unshakable faith and showed us the unseen side of life in all its splendor.

For nineteen years I have carried the MasterCard that Allison found in the elevator and the religious medal of Mary pinned inside my wallet. I hope someday to give them to Christopher.

* * *

A decade later, Allison, then happily married, gave birth to a son. It was then that I felt vindicated for not having realized that my daughter was pregnant ten years earlier. Allison never needed maternity clothes for her second pregnancy either. Both sons weighed more than eight pounds. Chip and I were once again with Allison for her labor and birth. This time, however, our grandson's birth was a very joyful occasion.

Allison works as a corporate manager with the same Fortune 500 company where she first discovered the Master-Card. Her son, now grown, was raised in the Roman Catholic faith. When my grandson made his first Holy Communion, I was unable to be there. The pictures Allison sent me of the procession just *happened* to be snapped when he was walking by the statue of the Virgin Mary that stands in front of his church.

Miraculous Medal found by Barbara

May 1979. The inscription reads

"O Mary! Conceived Without Sin

Pray for us who Have Recourse to Thee."

Christopher Robin

Oh, little one just newly born
Who from her womb has been torn
I will never see your baby face
Never know nor feel the grace
That God has bestowed on you.
Christopher Robin will you ever know
How much I want to hold you?
Will you ever know how much I miss you?
Will you ever know how much I love you?
My little bird, I'll think of you each spring
Whenever I see a robin nest.
I know your mom loved you so
She gave you up to have the best.
My firstborn grandchild you will always be
So very, very special to me.
No matter what you are called
No matter where you are lain
No matter when you come,
For I will see you again.
It may not be here on this earthly plane
Nor under skies of blue
But you and I have met before
And underneath the pain I bore
I knew you were not mine
But here for someone else divine.
Baby Christopher, will you come one day
To see me when I am old and gray?
If not, we will meet again to pray
In another time, another way.
I give you up with joy and pain
You were not to be an earthly gain
But a soul that was carried by one who knew
You were neither hers nor mine to view.

Over the years, Christopher was never far from my thoughts. I always prayed for him and his adoptive family, and I was always aware of the milestones that were being celebrated in his life... starting school, graduations, perhaps college or the military. I wondered about him always. What did he look like? Was he athletic like my sons? Did he like to swim as we all did?

My longing to meet him only increased with time; I was getting older and was fearful that I may never see him. One day I started to look for him under the name I knew he was given. The adoption papers were not to be found anywhere and the spelling of his last name was very unique; the closest I came was finding someone in Hawaii and I knew he was in another state. Faced with what seemed to be a dead end, I put aside my longing and went on with my busy life.

One day when looking for a legal document I found his adoption papers. It had a lot of information in that allowed me to locate him via the computer. Then I found a phone number. Could this possibly be his home?

A moment later, I found myself speaking with Christopher's adoptive father. I eagerly identified myself, and he told me many stories of my grandson's life. When we were about to hang up he said he would have his wife call me back. She never did, though she did mail me some pictures of him as a baby and a child. I did hear from his father again, when he called to tell me that Christopher was not interested in contacting his birth mother. It seemed I would have to make do with the photographs...or so I thought.

My prayers came true on October 2, 2007, the eve of my birthday. My husband, and I had just retired to the bedroom to read when the phone rang. As I reached over to answer it, Chip and I exchanged puzzled looks; it was unusually late for a phone call.

"Is this Barbara Harris?"

My initial reaction was that the deep voice sounded a bit like one of my two older sons.

"Yes..."

"This is Richard, your grandson."

My heart nearly leaped out of my chest!

"Christopher!" I screamed before I could stop myself.

He said he wanted me to know that I had a great-granddaughter named Elizabeth who had been christened that day in the Roman Catholic faith. Oh my God! Elizabeth—Chip's fond name for me—and she was Catholic! Immediately, my head began to spin with thoughts and questions.

"How Are You? Where are You?" I asked excitedly as the tears flowed freely down my cheeks and I let out sobs of relief that had been held in my heart for decades.

I looked over at Chip and saw that he too had tears streaming down his face. In our forty years together I had only seen my husband cry twice before: once, when our son-in-law died after being burned in an industrial accident, and the other when he came home after having to hand Christopher over to his adoptive parents. Now he was crying with tears of joy.

"I want to get in touch with my birth mother...," he said, then added haltingly, "Do you think she will want to speak to me? I want to thank her for giving birth to me...for giving me life!"

Would Allison talk to him? I did not know. I quickly reached for my cell phone and called her. I barely got out the words, "Christopher is on the other phone" when she cut me off with a "Yes, Yes, Yes!" and I quickly hung up so he could call her.

The rest, as they say, is history. A family reunion was arranged in our home. When I saw him, it was just like looking at one of my sons—he was the same height and broad-shouldered, with a cheerful countenance. The only difference was his beautiful green eyes that at this moment held years of emotion. To say that we rejoiced all weekend would be an understatement.

It was the beginning of a meaningful, close relationship that continues to this day. At the time of this writing, and ten years since that fateful phone call from Christopher, I visited Allison for our birthdays. I stayed with Amy, and we joined Richard and his wife for a picnic. When I went to greet his wife and give her a welcoming hug, she turned around and was obviously pregnant.

We were thrilled but concerned; they had lost a son a year earlier at his birth. The loss left us devastated. They named him Christopher Kyle. He will always live on in our hearts, our thoughts and our prayers.

We prayed together for this new life, and in January 2018 those prayers were answered when Richard and his wife welcomed a handsome, healthy baby boy into the world. As we all joined together in celebration, I thought back to that night so many years ago when Christopher was born, and how

I had to surrender and trust Mother Mary that all was going according to plan. Now, as I look at my first-born grandson and his family , my heart fills with joy, gratitude, and an absolute knowing that Mother Mary had spoken the truth.

"I prayed for this child, and the Lord has granted me what I asked of him."

1 Samuel 1-27

JOY!

The miracle happened tonight on the phone
It was you, Christopher now fully grown!
Will you ever know what that did for me?
It lengthened my life at least times three
Not just you- but a great-granddaughter too!
Can this be real? Is it happening? Is it true?
I listened as he recounted his life events
And now it was all making perfect sense
I had found him in Hawaii on that fated day
A wounded marine~ in a Veteran's hospital he lay
He would recover and go on to live his life
Not filled with knowledge of our stress or strife
How much he was loved and wanted by us all
But she had heard another Spiritual call
He now knew how much love filled her heart
When you and she that sad day had to part.

Chapter Five

MANIFESTING MOTHER MARY'S MESSAGE

*I*n my previous book, *Conversations with Mary,* I was given a mandate to tell of the sanctity of life.

Did this mean that I would have to discuss the abortion issue? I was vehemently opposed to doing so. When asked about my position on the issue, I always gave my stock answer: "I am personally against abortion but I support a woman's right to choose." It was an easy answer, one that satisfied myself, as well as my friends and colleagues. It required no thought and no one challenged me.

That said, as a result of my experiences—the joy of being an adoptive mother and the sorrow of surrendering my first grandchild—I am a strong advocate for life, and for adoption.

Over the course of my life, I have also been exposed to abortion experiences I reflected back on while writing this book.

Case I—A Young Nurses' Choice

It was 1953. I was a nineteen-year-old student nurse experiencing my three-month rotation in the operating room. One morning I was assigned to be the first circulating nurse, which meant I would assist the scrub nurse, who was assisting the surgeon. A registered nurse on staff was supervising me. Judging from my previous observations I believed this would be an easy assignment for me.

I knew nothing about the patient or the case. Just enough to say hello, check for the "permission to operate" signatures and make sure that her diamond wedding ring was tied to her wrist with gauze. I thought this was to be a "D&C"—or dilation and curettage of the uterine wall. This procedure was done routinely for women with various gynecological problems, but unbeknownst to me this morning would be different. As I stood there watching the surgeon, I saw a large piece of tissue and blood drop down into the pail. This would be mine to clean up after the procedure was over.

When the surgeon was finished, everyone quickly left and I hurried about my tasks as another surgery was scheduled for that room. I bent down to gather the tissue for laboratory examination, and what I saw left a permanent scar on my soul. For there in the pail was a tiny, fully formed baby. My God! I thought I would faint.

"Oh," I cried out to the air, "look at those precious little fingers and toes." I froze in fear, nausea now overcoming me. Tears welled in my eyes and began to run down my cheeks. One of the staff nurses who was passing by saw me sitting on the surgeon's stool, crying. I was devastated.

"What's the matter?" she asked solicitously. I could not speak but shakily pointed to the pail.

"Oh, go see the supervisor," she said casually, "This is a therapeutic abortion. You don't have to assist on those." She then gave me a little hug. "Go ahead, I'll clean it up for you."

Still tearful, I sought out the operating supervisor, a nurse I greatly admired.

"What's the matter, kid?" she asked in her direct manner.

"I just saw a little baby in a pail and I cannot stand it," I said, chin quivering.

She beckoned me into her office. "Are you Catholic?" she asked.

"No," I replied, "I am a Methodist."

"Then you must assist on these cases. Only Catholics are exempt."

"Then I cannot be a nurse," I said with finality, "I will have to leave school."

"Oh, no, I don't want you to do that. You are going to be a great nurse. If it bothers you that much you I won't assign you in the future." She pointed a finger at my chest as she added, "I don't want any further discussion of this matter."

And that was that. I wouldn't give this traumatic event another thought until ten years later, when the issue of abortion would hit much closer to home.

Case II—A Mother's Choice

My next experience with abortion occurred when I was pregnant with my fourth child, Michael. As I wrote about earlier, this was a deeply desired, planned pregnancy by myself and my husband. An early routine X-ray showed our son to be in an unusual position. His limbs were spread out as if in a celebratory dance instead of fetal position.

My obstetrician talked with me about the possible causes. One was that his brain was open and was draining spinal fluid into my uterus. He said I had a condition called *poly-hydramnios,* which meant my placenta was producing too much fluid. I would have to visit the operating room periodically to be "drained" by an incision through my abdomen and into the womb. This procedure was both frightening and painful because anesthesia was not administered for the sake of our child.

I talked with my husband about our options. Abortion was one of them. As a physician and a nurse, we knew the odds of having a healthy baby.

"It's your call," John said.

Just then my mind flashed back to those precious little hands and feet I had seen in the pail ten years earlier. There was not even a moment's doubt for me. I would *not* have an abortion. I would have our baby. I intuitively knew Michael would be fine, and I held onto that thought throughout the difficult pregnancy. I could not sleep in a bed, as the excess fluid made it difficult to breathe. Instead we purchased a reclining chair, which is where I slept in an upright position for the last few months.

Michael appeared on the scene almost five weeks early on a beautiful Palm Sunday morning. He weighed six pounds, two ounces; a wonderful weight for an infant of that gestation period. He was a darling baby and after an initial, momentary scare he proclaimed his arrival, with a loud, healthy wail. Though it was never a serious consideration, I shuddered to think what we would have missed had we made a different choice.

Case III—A Case of No Choice

I had another experience with abortion, one so painful that I had buried it deep in my psyche for many years. It was the late 1980s, and I was working as a psychiatric nurse in the dual-diagnosis adolescent unit of a famous hospital. I had chosen this specialty when I returned to the nursing profession after my children were older. I loved the adolescents and I loved my work.

One evening, when I reported to the unit, the charge nurse said to me, "You don't need to listen to report tonight." At my questioning stare she added mysteriously, "I want you to "special" a patient in the Quiet Room."

"Special" meant I would sit with one patient for eight hours. I thought this odd because the youngsters who were placed in the Quiet Room were there for disciplinary reasons. They were usually assigned to a strong, male, psychiatric technician because of the physical danger involved.

"What is the problem?" I asked suspiciously.

"Oh, it's Lorraine," she answered quietly. "She was taken out by her parents for an 'a-b' today. She just returned and is very upset."

I was astounded! Lorraine was fifteen years old and "a-b" meant abortion. This was certainly no place for a postoperative patient. What if she hemorrhages? My head spinning, I quickly grabbed my stethoscope and blood-pressure cuff and ran down the hallway. Before I reached the room I could hear her screams.

Lorraine was lying on a mattress in the small, white eight-by-ten Quiet Room. She clutched her pillow to her abdomen. Her curly blonde hair, wet with sweat, clung to her face. Periodically, she would let out an ear-piercing scream at the top of her lungs, followed by a mournful howl. "They killed my baby! They killed my baby." Then she would break into deep sobs.

I approached her gently.

"Lorraine, it's Bobbi. I'm here to take care of you," I said softly while slowly offering my hand to her.

"Don't touch me!" she screamed as she crawled on her hands and knees to the corner of the room and cowered like a frightened animal. "Don't come near me! I don't want you to take my baby again. Don't kill her again!" She sounded terrified.

God, I have to do something, I thought. *But what?* I began to pray and ask for guidance.

"Lorraine, I am here to help you, "I said softly while slowly inching my way to her corner. As if in answer to my prayer, I began to sing:

> *Jesus loves me, this I know,*
>
> *for the Bible tells me so.*
>
> *Little ones to him belong;*
>
> *they are weak but He is strong.*
>
> *Yes, Jesus loves me, yes, Jesus loves me...*

Where did that hymn come from? I think Lorraine is Jewish. I hope she won't mind... after all, Jesus was Jewish! My thoughts were racing now. Nevertheless, I continued to sing this verse over and over very softly. Lorraine's screams gradually subsided. Meanwhile, I slowly sank down on the mattress to be closer to her.

"Why don't you come over here and let me sing to you? Come on, Lorrie, I won't hurt you, I will rock you," I said gently.

Slowly she crawled over the mattress and fell into my arms. I cradled this young child and began to sing softly. It was the same "homemade lullaby" that I had sung to my own children.

> *Mommy's little baby.*
>
> *Mommy's little girl.*
>
> *I love Mommy's baby.*
>
> *Mommy loves her girl.*

Soon Lorraine was quiet. Only an occasional sob escaped.

"I have to check you for bleeding," I said quietly.

"Don't hurt me," she whimpered.

"I won't."

I also took her blood pressure, relieved to find it in normal range. When I was finished with my cursory examination, she crawled back into my arms and I continued to sing and rock her.

She cried and said over and over, "They killed my baby. They didn't even tell me what they were doing. I didn't even know anything until it was over."

I wept right along with her, and I realized that beneath

the sorrow I was incredibly angry at what this young girl had been put through.

I sat on the floor with Lorraine for eight hours rocking her as a mother would rock her own child. It was during this period that Lorraine told me she'd wanted to give her baby up for adoption. She had it all planned. She could bring happiness to someone else. Her life would then have meaning. This pregnancy would not be in vain. As I listened to her—and thought of my own experiences on both the receiving and giving end of adoption—I grew angrier still; in fact, I was enraged. Why had no one served as the unborn child's advocate? As Lorraine's?

"No," I was later informed by the social workers, "neither of them had any rights."

To me, that did not seem just. Lorraine remained under treatment in the hospital for more than a month. The night nurses reported that she would wake up screaming and crying, "They killed my baby."

My heart ached for her, and for the others who would surely follow, for this was not the first nor the last teenager to have an abortion against her will. I am sure Lorraine will bear this scar for the rest of her life.

Even now, decades later, my heart is hurting and tears sting my eyes as I write this. It is my fervent prayer that women who find themselves with an unwanted pregnancy will seek counseling to surrender their baby for adoption.

Chapter Six

MANIFESTING HEAVEN

A baby! A darling cherub was smiling at me, and I reached out for him. It was Christopher. Just as I was about to hold him someone snatched him out of my arms. It was at that moment I awakened from the dream with severe chest pain. A second later everything went black, and when I awoke again I was in an ambulance. Chip had called the rescue squad when he was unable to rouse me.

Like most medical professionals, I was ill-prepared to be a patient. As I lay there in the ambulance, feeling frightened and alone, out of control and powerless, my analytical mind switched on, trying to find reasons for my predicament.

Did the severe pain stem from the heartbreak of losing my first grandchild? I suspected this was the case. An early fan of metaphysician, Dr. Louise L. Hay, I knew emotional pain could convert to physical ailments. Though four years had passed since Christopher's adoptive parents took him away, the emotions had been trapped in my heart ever since. Now, I believed, they landed me in the emergency room.

When I met Dr. Mason, the cardiologist on call, I immediately liked him. Friendly and handsome in a Huck Finn sort way, this man whom I guessed to be about 40, looked like he'd be more at home with a fishing pole than a stethoscope. I decided I would tell him about my dream; I was certain that once he heard it—and its significance in my life—he would agree with my theory.

Boy, was I wrong! I had barely gotten the words out of my mouth when he quickly dismissed the idea. Rather than empathizing and exploring the family's loss of Christopher, he admitted me to the hospital at once for a cardiac catheterization, a procedure whereby a tube is inserted through an artery leading to the heart to assess any blockages or damage. This was the small community hospital where Christopher was born. I had not been there since that day. My present experience was not lessening my grief.

"I had a patient just like you last month," he said repeatedly, as if trying to convince me I was wrong to connect my emotional and physical pain. "She's also a nurse, same symptoms, same age, and her arteries were completely blocked. You know, she even looks like you. We saved her life."

He was so certain of his diagnosis, he went ahead and reserved a bed in a large city hospital nearby where heart surgery was regularly performed.

"I am not that nurse!" I cried. "I am me!" My protests fell on deaf ears. I was not a happy camper. I talked once more to Dr. Mason about my theory of the etiology of my chest pain.

"You're in denial," Mason solemnly informed me. "Denial is common among nurses. You think you're invincible!" he added.

"Why won't you listen to me about Christopher?" I pleaded.

Then my rational, medically trained mind took over. I

decided perhaps something *was* wrong. At my relatively young age, I knew it was rare, but I certainly *could* have blocked arteries and heart surgery *would* save my life. Though still reluctant to accept the medical possibilities, I surrendered.

I know you are in charge, God, I prayed. I *know this is for a reason. Please protect me during this procedure.* An answer came back in the small, loving inner voice I had known since childhood: *There is a higher purpose for this holiday hospitalization,* it said simply.

Trusting implicitly in the answer, I signed the legal release form, though I did wonder what that higher purpose might be.

I remembered remarking to my husband a week earlier that I felt suspended, but calm, waiting for something to happen. It was a feeling I had never experienced before. Was the hospitalization what I had intuitively anticipated, even though I was enjoying excellent health?

"Anything is possible," I answered myself, and picked up a book to pass the time while I waited for the test.

But my peaceful wait was not to be. I was suddenly gripped by a wave of anticipatory anxiety. Every muscle in my body went into spasm and it felt as if I was wearing a suit of armor. In retrospect I think I was "armoring" myself for the heart catheterization.

I rang for the nurse. She appeared quickly, but acted very annoyed.

"What's goin' on?" she asked, while roughly picking up my arm to check my pulse.

"I don't know. Maybe I'm having a reaction to the medication you gave me." By now my body was painfully arched backwards and my feet were reaching for the back of my head.

"I'll call the doctor right away and have him order a muscle relaxant or a mild tranquilizer," she said sharply.

"Okay, but it seems to me some drug must be irritating the central nervous system," I said.

"Could be," she answered brusquely and left my bedside.

What is the matter with her? I thought. *She is so nasty and short of patience.* When she returned with my medication I asked her if she was feeling stressed from the large number of critically ill patients in the unit. I wanted her to know I understood—I had walked in her shoes.

Immediately, her demeanor changed. "No," she replied sadly, "this is my first evening back on duty in almost six weeks. My seventeen-year- old daughter went into a coma from mixing alcohol and drugs at a party." She paused, trying to retain her composure. "The doctors don't think she will ever come out of it."

Oh, how my heart went out to her!

She left a few minutes later to go about her other duties, but throughout her shift she popped in and out of my room to talk about her daughter. I had given her a space and an outlet to express her feelings. At the same time, my concern for her took my mind off my own pain and the approaching procedure. I realized that we all have spiritual tests on the earthly plane. I was not alone in my grief. There were others with more to grieve than I. At least Christopher was alive and with a good family. I was sure God had perfectly placed this nurse with me to again demonstrate that lesson.

After my restless night, a hospital aide brought me to a small room in preparation for the cardiac catheterization. A friendly nurse helped me onto a black table that was cold and hard. I could hear the operating team scrubbing their hands. I was scared silly. As I looked around the room, I noticed that the walls were painted my favorite, peaceful sky blue. I then noticed rows of musical tape cassettes that were stored in a wooden holder against the opposite wall.

"I love music," I said to the nurse readying me for the test.

Dr. Mason suddenly appeared next to the table and began a lively conversation.

"So you like music. Do you have the old Mario Lanza Christmas recording? It is my favorite. How 'bout Tennessee Ernie Ford and Perry Como?" he asked in rapid-fire succession.

"Yes, I have them all. I like Nat King Cole the best," I replied. We laughed, enjoying the musical memories and the camaraderie.

"Would you like some music played during your procedure?" the nurse asked.

"You bet. I would love that," I answered.

"What do you want to hear?"

"Oh, why don't you pick out a tape?" I answered, suddenly sleepy. "I'll enjoy anything."

"You trust my judgment?" she asked playfully.

"I sure do!"

"Okay, here we go." She slid the selected tape into the recorder.

The small room was soon filled with the dulcet tones of Johnny Mathis. I could not believe what I was hearing! It was "The Twelfth of Never," a song about eternal love. This was "our" song, Chip's and mine, and Johnny Mathis's rendition was our favorite. I was astounded by the synchronicity! My chin quivered uncontrollably and the sobs escaped.

"Barbara," Dr. Mason asked. "Tell me, what is the matter?"

My throat was so tight I could barely answer. Embarrassed, I finally managed to explain.

"What are the odds of that song being picked?" I asked between my sobs. The doctor and nurses, peering at each other over their surgical masks, looked visibly shaken.

One nurse took my hand. "It's okay, it's okay," she said, but her words seemed more directed at herself than at me.

No, it's not okay! I screamed silently. Knowing I had to get control of my emotions before they began the procedure, I employed a favorite device I had developed over the years. I yelled, "Stop it!" while visualizing a red stop sign.

The doctor and the nurses jumped in alarm when I called out, but my method worked. As always, I calmed down immediately. I then explained what I had done. The eyes behind the masks looked puzzled—this was the early 1980s and it was obvious that no one in the room had heard about creative visualization.

"Do you want me to change the music?" Dr. Mason asked.

"Oh, no," I answered without hesitation. "I love this song. It's a good sign. My husband couldn't come into the operating room, so the music means he's here with me in spirit." That thought comforted me but seemed unsettling to the staff.

"Something wonderful is going to happen today," I added. "I know that my heart is going to be okay."

"Don't get your hopes up," he responded cautiously; then he glanced at the nurses and added, "Let's get this show on the road."

"I'm ready to go," I replied. I had no idea how prophetic my words would be.

As the staff began the procedure, I listened to the music and focused on the words of the song: "...love you till the poets run out of rhyme . . . and that's a long, long time." The marvelous melody and lilting lyrics comforted my soul.

"What's the date?" I asked, suddenly having a thought.

After a moment, a nurse replied, "The eleventh?"

"No," I said, "I think it's the twelfth, the twelfth of December, isn't it? What synchronicity!"

I laughed, enjoying the intrigue immensely.

"Barbara," a nurse said in her best soothe-the-patient voice, "it is the eleventh of December. Now get hold of yourself!"

The sedative relaxed me, and I could feel the catheter

enter my femoral artery. Craning my neck to see the television monitor, I saw the tube inching up to my heart. It looked like a big worm crawling inside my body. Then the image of my heart appeared on the TV screen. This really was cool! What a privilege it was to see my own heart beating within my body.

"Look!" I called out. "My arteries are clear. They look just like a teenager's!"

They were just as I had imagined. I was thrilled.

The next memory I had was of a large, swirling black cloud of enormous power and energy enveloping me. I was surrounded by a roar similar to a freight train thundering down the tracks. The black energy encircled me, and the operating room slowly dimmed. I experienced no pain as I felt gently lifted from the table, like a child in the arms of her father.

Then I seemed to travel headfirst, with my hands outstretched in front of me, as if preparing for a dive off the edge of a swimming pool. *Like Wendy and Peter Pan*, I thought. Though tornado-like forces spun around me I felt peaceful, engulfed by love.

Lights blinked to my right and left. I wondered if they were other souls also traveling at breakneck speed down the long, dark tunnel of whirling energy. Some lights seemed stuck to the sides of this whirling cyclone of energy, rather than traveling forward.

Is that hell? I wondered, *being lodged in this tunnel, assaulted by a cacophony of sound while others soar past?*

I could not know. For me, this trip was warm, wonderful,

and serene with neither fear nor pain. Wrapped in a warm cocoon of light, I was unconcerned about my destination. Cast out of the tunnel, I found myself suspended in a brilliant, loving light without dimension. Its every molecule spoke silently of love. Glorious, otherworldly colors were everywhere. Pinks, golds, mauves, lavenders, blues, greens and magentas—all more luminous than anything I have ever seen on earth—swirled around me. They, too, communicated love. I suddenly knew color would be used to heal on the earthly plane. It had been used before, yet this knowledge was forgotten.

Magnificent flowers of infinite varieties and indescribable colors were everywhere. Most of them I had never seen before. The rose seemed to occupy an exalted position among all of the flowers. Maybe that was because it was my favorite. I remembered thinking the use of flowers for healing was another forgotten body of knowledge.

Heavenly, soul inspiring, brilliant music seemed to emanate from the flowers. Was this possible? Music was everywhere! The term "music of the spheres" came to mind, and I understood what it meant.

The knowledge came to me that our thoughts initiate all creation, including disease, and that all memories are stored like genetic material in every cell and are passed down from generation to generation. I was told that loving touch given by a caring person can release these cellular memories.

I remember looking at Earth. It was but a small part of the picture. The planet was surrounded by a heavenly blue haze and guarded by very large angels. While viewing these scenes, I was simultaneously looking at my physical body lying on the operating table. Dr. Mason and the nurses, their voices raised, were administering electrical shock to my heart. I saw the large steel paddles being used on my convulsing body.

What is the message, I wondered? I still don't know. Everyone appeared frantic but I was emotionally removed from the scene. My physical body lying there lifeless meant nothing to me. Actually, I felt much lighter after discarding it; in fact, I was more clearly the essence of myself than ever before.

Incredibly, I had no thoughts of my beloved husband or my cherished children and grandchildren. Nor did I miss them. Instead I felt that I had finally come back to my rightful place. I had at last reached home, and the understanding brought me profound peace.

Where are the angels? I wondered, looking around. *Where is heaven?* I asked no one in particular.

Heaven is in your heart, came the answer from a voice beyond.

Who is speaking? I asked.

It is I, Mother Mary, responded a firm, welcoming voice.

I was not surprised to hear her, I simply searched to connect the voice with an image. I could only see an angular jawline, which I thought belonged to a man. Then I realized I was looking at a female whose nature was strong. The jaw slowly connected to a face. Most of all I remember the eyes. They were almost clear but at the same time, blue, green and violet.

You must go back, she said, transmitting her words by thought. *Your work is not finished.*

No, I replied, *I do not want to go back.*

You must go back into nursing, she admonished. *You are a healer. You have been given a mission. Nursing is your forum for sharing what you have learned here.*

I gazed at Mother Mary in all her splendor. She stood tall and erect; her facial expression, the most compassionate and pure I had ever gazed upon. Her body radiated a brilliant white light intermingled with the most dazzling of colors. Mary's robe was a pale rose. I had always thought of her as wearing blue.

Why do you wear a rose-colored gown? I asked.

She answered as if talking to a child. *My robe's color emanates from within, from my essence. There is no light reflection, as there is no sun here. The color rose represents a mother or father's unconditional love and it is the color of God's love for you. Remember this lesson. Love is the only thing that matters. You will go back and, as a healer, teach of love.*

Standing with her right arm outstretched, she both pointed the way back and blessed me. Her other arm encircled the shoulders of a beautiful little girl with long blonde hair. I recognized the child as the daughter of a dear childhood friend. Her death at four years of age had been one of the most painful experiences of my life.

No, no, I do not want to go back.

Go now, my child. Go in peace, she told me gently but

with finality. *You will come back when it is your time. I will be waiting for you. I will also contact you as need requires I do so.*

I don't want to leave, I pleaded, *I am home.*

Bless you, my child, she answered and faded from view.

In the blink of an eye, I traveled with breakneck speed down through the tunnel and reentered my physical body. I remember being there for just a nanosecond. Then I left again. Considering how much I wanted to stay with Mary I was not surprised by my quick abandonment of the physical realm. I also was never one to accept the first no for an answer.

Once again, I viewed the doctor and nurses applying electric shock to my heart and my convulsing body.

Stop! Oh no! My chest is going to be burned, I shouted at them. They, of course, could not hear me.

The second trip was almost identical to the first. The tunnel, the incredible light, the magnificent colors, and the heavenly music were all there. But Mother Mary was nowhere to be found.

Instead, I was met by a very large angel with a huge wingspan He identified himself to me as Michael the Archangel. His voice, just like Mary's, was transmitted by thought. There was no need to speak here. Later I was told this is called "an impress." His demeanor was kind but firm. He seemed to be guarding a door but bade me to enter. I found myself in a large library that held no books but offered access to all knowledge.

The knowledge of the universe is available to all who

seek it, he said in thought. He then gestured to my right, where an infinite room with no walls, floor, or ceiling spread out before me. I then understood that this was where mere mortals could obtain information we had not learned or experienced on the earthly plane. I remember thinking that this is what Mozart had done; what child prodigies do.

"Go back," the angel said. *"You have much work to do."*

Then he vanished, and the Blessed Mother appeared again, this time above me.

I have visited and supported you during your grief, she said. *I spoke to you during the birth of your first grandchild, Christopher. It is no coincidence he was divinely named for my son Jesus and renamed Richard by his adoptive parents. The name means strong, hardy, powerful, a leader.*

This was all as preplanned. You must go back, my child, and complete your work. I know you are tired, but you must reenter nursing. You are a healer. You will teach about thought and the interconnection of all things.

When you return to the nursing profession, she continued, *you will be part of a heavenly-led movement. We have selected the nurses to lead the world into the next century because they have always been filled with love. Now they have been given much knowledge and will be writing many healing books. They will need the help of souls such as you. You will assist in the transition of nursing into the next millennium. Now go in peace.*

Though I heard the words, I did not comprehend their importance. Like a child being torn from her mother's womb, I reached out and screamed her name, *No, no, Mother Mary, please, I want to stay!*

Reaching out her right hand in a loving gesture, she blessed me and directed me back. She then faded gradually from view. I wept.

The next memory I had was reentry into my physical body. I saw a group of Nazi soldiers standing over my physical body and performing what I perceived as surgery. I awakened myself with a bloodcurdling scream. To this day I do not know the meaning of that vision.

"Mary, Mary! Are you the Virgin Mary?" I asked the figure slowly coming into my vision. She was not dressed in a rose-colored robe.

"No, I am not Mary," the nurse said cheerfully. "I'm Peggy and I'm not even a virgin." Everyone in the room laughed. It was clearly a relief.

"I'm not in heaven?" I asked.

"No, you're in the hospital," Dr. Mason replied.

Suddenly, I was oriented—back in my physical body. Something had hit me very hard in the chest. The pain was excruciating. I looked down and saw the burns there.

"Did you hit me with a bat?"

"No," the nurse replied. "You...."

Before Peggy finished speaking, I realized I'd had a near-death experience in that operating room. Having been on the other end of such an event, I knew the anguish Dr. Mason and the nurses had suffered while trying to save me.

"Oh, no, I'm sorry. I'm so sorry," I said over and over

again.

"Are you all right?" Dr. Mason asked, bending over me and placing a solicitous hand on my shoulder.

"Yes, yes," I replied. "Oh, something fantastic happened to me," I said hurriedly and enthusiastically. "I can't wait to tell you!"

"Oh, no you don't!" he said suddenly thrusting his hand up in a "stop position" between our bodies. "You just turned my hair gray! I don't want to hear about anything right now. I'm gonna sit down. I'm just so happy to see you talking."

"Well, okay," I said, disappointed but now fully understanding what fear he must have experienced. Turning to Peggy I said excitedly, "I went into a tunnel and saw the Blessed Virgin Mary!"

"I don't care where you went or what you saw," she responded good-naturedly. "I'm just thankful you're back here." She reached over and stroked my head. "You're suffering from shock. Those memories will fade."

At that moment, I wisely decided to record what had happened to me and not to discuss the events with anyone except my husband.

Strolling over to the audio tapes, Peggy selected another and popped it in the machine. A second later the room soon resounded with yet another song my husband and I played over and over while courting— "El Condor Pasa."

I listened to the words— "I'd rather be a hammer than a nail…"—and burst out laughing.

"Don't tell me that is another one of your songs," Peg

said mockingly.

I chuckled. "Yes, and it's a long, long story."

"I'm going to take you back to your room now," she said as if she couldn't wait to get me out of the operating room.

As she pushed my stretcher to the elevator, I suddenly remembered my earlier question. "Oh, by the way, what's the date?"

"It's the twelfth of December," Peggy answered. "You were right, after all."

"Why did you lie to me?" I felt betrayed.

"Because you really spooked us," she answered frankly. "If I were you, I wouldn't worry about anything you saw or experienced. Just remember, this too shall pass."

A chill ran up and down my spine and the hair on my arms stood on end. I was silent with my memories. "This too shall pass" had been my mother's favorite saying. She had made her permanent trip to the "other side" on July 3, 1982. Before she died, I crawled into her hospital bed with her, held her in my arms, and rocked her.

Looking up at me with her beautiful blue eyes, faded with age, she said, "I just want to go home."

"Do you mean to heaven?" I asked.

"Yes. When I say that to the doctors and nurses," she added in disgust, "they think I mean I want to go home to my house."

Oh, how I wish I had been fortunate to see my mother during my trip, for it was she who taught me to understand that faith is more important than religion. I went over and over this event in my mind during the next twelve hours while I was required to lie flat on my back with a ten-pound bag of sand on my femoral artery.

I had survived what is now known as a near-death experience (NDE). Why hadn't the doctor and nurses wanted to hear about it? I guess a new thought or the possibility that there truly was an afterlife was frightening to them.

I was overjoyed when Chip walked into my room. It felt as though I hadn't seen him in days.

"What did the doctor tell you?" I asked.

"Oh, he said you were fine. He also said something about having to 'jump-start' you twice." Chip gave me a puzzled look. "What was that all about? I asked Dr. Mason what he meant, and he said not to worry about it."

He then reached for my hand and bent down and kissed me.

He had to jump-start me twice! What was I? An old Ford motor car! I was incensed about the doctor's casual explanation and proceeded to relate my wondrous tale to my husband. Three days later I would put pen to paper, recording it for posterity. I never expected to tell another soul.

***

Now I have glimpsed "home" and I long to return there someday. Even now as I write these words my eyes fill with tears. I still yearn for the peace and tranquility I experienced. I long to be back in Mother Mary's presence. I am also astounded that I did not want to return back to my body to live what I consider to be a wonderful life.

As directed, I left the real estate industry and returned to nursing.

I later learned that December 12th, the day of my NDE, is the celebrated Feast Day in the Roman Catholic Church, USA, to honor Our Lady of Guadalupe, the Patroness of the Americas. She is named for Mother Mary's appearance to Juan Diego north of Mexico City in 1531. A permanent image of this vision mysteriously appeared on his mantle.

***

The public view of Near Death Experiences (NDEs) has changed dramatically in the years since my trip to the other side. In fact, they are now considered common. Yet, though thousands of people have claimed to have experienced a Near Death Experiences, researchers remain polarized. One opinion holds that NDEs are caused by changes in the brain's chemistry and are therefore essentially meaningless.

Others believe that NDEs literally provide a glimpse of the afterlife or of God or other religious figures. Many books have been written and movies made on the subject, which in turn encourages others to come forward and speak of their experiences. The vast majority contend that their lives were dramatically changed by their NDE, with some struggling with having to be here after seeing the incredible beauty of the other side, while others feel their lives have improved considerably.

I believe the increased acceptance of NDEs is due in part to the several physicians who claim to have had them. The most noted is a neurosurgeon, Dr. Eben Alexander, whose brain was attacked by a rare meningitis caused by E. coli., When he recovered he wrote the book *Proof of Heaven,* a riveting account of his experience, including detailed adventures and encounters he had on the other side. It also reveals personal family information he returned with after his NDE—information he could not possibly have known any other way.

Of course, the skeptics ignore this because they say his coma was medically induced and he was hallucinating. When will their eyes open to new horizons? When will they look back and see that most of our progress in science was at one time considered impossible?

These are the same scientists who debunked the theory that *thought* could affect our health and even help people recover from many disabling syndromes. Then enlightened neurologists proved them wrong, as did Annie Hopper, a Canadian counselor whose life was destroyed by Chemical Sensitivity Syndrome. She has developed a program to help people retrain their neural pathways.

These enlightened medical explorers believe in "neuroplasticity." It is the brain's ability to form new neural pathways and heal many syndromes through the limbic system. We are at a new frontier in the brain's capabilities, as it has trillions of cells yet unused.

It reminds me of so many of our wonderful scientists in the past who developed many techniques and inventions thought to be impossible ... they too were scoffed at by their colleagues!

"When you live your life with an appreciation of coincidences and their meanings,

you connect with the underlying field of infinite possibilities.

This is when the magic begins."

~Deepak Chopra

Meeting Mother Mary

Traveling down the tunnel that day
Leaving my earthly body, I pray
To see what heaven is about
To learn of God and Saints, no doubt
Instead a being of another kind
A woman so lovely she brought to mind
The times when I had seen her before.
"Are you Mary?" I asked at the door
"Yes," she replied countenance filled with love
" 'Tis I who has given you a glimpse of above"
"Go back now," she silently bade
"Weep no more, be not afraid."
Blessing me with an ivory glove
Dismissed, now soaring like a dove
Returning to the earth once more
Beckoning again, turned away at the door.
There never can be a worldly gain
To match the splendor of the heavenly plane..

What Is Love?

DID I LOVE ENOUGH? stated simply as can be
That was the question asked of me.
When I gasped my last breath that December morn
Just like the first breath... when I was born
A profound sense of awe came over me
When I understood how simple life could be.
Not speaking about Love...the romantic kind
Nor shiny rings or ties that bind.
Not the games between a gal and a guy.
For many of those will end with a sigh.
It reaches far deeper than that illusion
The stuff that causes so much confusion
The Love that I am speaking of
Is carried on the wings of a soaring dove
It is love for mankind; its highest form
One I wish was the norm.
It's the kind of love shown everyday
To those we meet at work and play.
Know that life is not about the race
To gather and do things at a rapid pace
It's about those you helped along the way
Love is making someone's life a better day.

Chapter Seven

MANIFESTING THE NEGATIVE

*"Once you replace negative thoughts
with positive ones,*

You'll start having positive results."

~Willie Nelson

I believe my interest in manifesting began following the surrender of my grandson for adoption and increased upon the adoption of my daughter. However, after my Near Death Experience (NDE) that curiosity and interest in the subject increased tenfold. I began to search for explanations on the subject and read every book I could find that mentioned the subject. This reading led me to quantum physics, which I still struggle to understand. However, I believe it is strongly linked to what I am manifesting.

I became a fan of Mike Dooley, a prolific author on this subject. To this day I belong to his unique organization and receive his daily message of Totally Unique Thoughts. (TUT) from his web site. He is truly one whose life is full of manifestations and his belief in it has encouraged many like me who are neophytes in manifesting.

In the years since then I have gone from being a healthy

skeptic to someone who knows that manifesting is as real as is the placement and movement of persons, places and things.

What I also realized was that words have power and one has to be very careful with their spoken words. The "be careful what you wish for" was shown to be a truism. As I observed people in my life I knew that many negative events in a person's life happened because they were spoken first.

One evening my husband and I became unwilling participants in an interesting example of this aspect of the Law of Attraction and The Power of Thought. It was an exciting time for us. After thirty-plus years with a major telecommunications firm, Chip was about to retire, and he and I were going to move to Florida.

One evening over dinner we were discussing his retirement, specifically what he wished to say to the people who had worked for and with him during his long, successful career.

Suddenly, he told me that his biggest fear was that someone would have a heart attack during his farewell speech.

"What in the world would make you think of that?" I asked incredulously.

He could not explain it, and I took the opportunity to talk about thought and its powerful impact on events. At that time Chip was a newcomer to this philosophy of positive affirmations and manifesting. I was slowly bringing him around to realizing the Power of Words but he was still a bit skeptical.

"I did not think of it..." he said firmly after my little speech, "the thought just kinda appeared in my mind. It made me wonder what it was all about!" I told him he could control and reframe the thought and bring about another outcome but he kind of brushed aside that idea.

Finally, the night both of us had waited for arrived. Chip stood up on the stage looking so handsome in his three-piece, pin-striped suit...it was the perfect farewell to the corporate rat race, and the beginning of our new life in Florida.

I was so proud of him as people called out, "Hey, Chip! Love you!" and "Going to Miss You!" Some began to applaud and soon all the crowd rose to their feet in a standing ovation. Chip humbly waited a moment, then asked them to be seated.

Just as he started his speech a male voice shouted out loudly, "We need a doctor or a nurse over here right now!"

I held back a moment to see if someone else might run to his aide, as there were over a hundred people in the room. But no one moved.

As I jumped up and ran toward the commotion I couldn't help but think, *Oh, no! I have on my new winter white suit!*

I am only human, after all!

The thought was replaced with concern when I saw the man lying unresponsive on the floor. I quickly assessed him and realized that he needed CPR. Now I was thinking, *Phew! Glad I just finished my recertification!*

After making sure someone had called for an ambulance I enlisted the help of a bystander and told everyone else to stand back to give me room to work.

It felt like my partner and I were there forever, alternately pumping and breathing for the man. At one point I thumped on his chest because he appeared to stop breathing again. My reactions were just second nature...no thinking is involved in that kind of situation. One just goes into robotic action as if guided. Finally, the medics arrived and took over.

Luckily, it was not a heart attack; the man had experienced a reaction to his medication mixed with alcohol. His heart was intact and he was only in the hospital overnight. He later sent me a beautiful large glass jar with a garden inside, along with a note about saving his life. I had done no such thing...it was just not his time to go.

My husband had learned a very valuable, albeit disturbing, lesson that night. When we discussed it after the party he asked me, "Do you think that was a result of my thinking about it? Did I attract it by giving the thought attention?"

I was fairly certain that it was but I did not dwell on the cause. If nothing else, the experience had opened his eyes to metaphysical things he'd never before considered! It had raised his awareness which is the first step to recognizing life's miracles!

We both agreed that regardless of the answer it was important to be aware of what you think and speak, for as was proven to us that night, our thoughts and words can certainly attract and manifest the negative!

Needless to say, Chip became a quick convert; he began paying closer attention to his thoughts and read up on The Law of Attraction. He also began to study the subject of The Law of Attraction and the subject of Manifestation.

Shortly after his retirement, we went out to dinner with

some very close friends. It was a bittersweet occasion, doubling as a celebration of his retirement and a farewell to them before we left the state.

The conversation eventually turned to what had happened the night of Chip's retirement dinner, which led to some deep philosophical discussions. I then related an event that had happened to me on a recent cross-country flight from California.

There was a woman sitting on the aisle, one row behind me on the opposite side of the plane. I noticed her because she was beautifully dressed. It was one of the few times we had flown first class.

Suddenly, from the corner of my eye, I saw the woman choking. No one else seemed to notice, though she was clearly in distress. I jumped up and did the Heimlich maneuver, dislodging the food stuck in her airway. As anyone who has experienced this knows, it flew out with quite a force. She was just fine once the food was out and after hugging and thanking me, she explained that she was on her way to her daughter's wedding and recently had surgery for cancer of the jaw!

After these events occur—and they seem to be happening more frequently—I always feel very shaky and have to center and breathe. I then give a quick prayer of gratitude to Spirit and the angels and archangels who I know are assisting me.

Our friends listened to my story. They were both highly educated, intellectual people with open minds – he was a VP of Marketing at a major corporation, and she was an accomplished, bright young woman who had a pilot's license and sold jet planes for a living. We'd often had many interesting conversations with them, and this evening was no different. Soon, a philosophical discussion about the choking events began.

They were having a strong difference of opinion about my experiences. The husband, who was agnostic, contended that because of my nurses' training my awareness was raised and that was why these events were happening to me. She, who was very spiritual, believed that it was Spirit/God who had placed me in the right and perfect spot *because* of my education and training.

Chip thought it was probably a combination of both and was trying to serve as mediator and peacekeeper.

Listening to this banter back and forth was very intriguing for me, as I was also wondering about these choking events which were taking place more frequently.

All of a sudden something made me look up, and what I saw truly shocked me. In a booth on the other side of the room there was a man choking! I noted the large steak on his plate and assumed he had a piece of steak stuck in his throat.

I catapulted out of my seat and rushed to the booth and got behind him and did the Heimlich maneuver and the steak flew out of his mouth. I was shaking again as usual and walked slowly back to our booth.

"Okay!" said our VP friend good-naturedly, "I surrender" and his wife said, "I rest my case!"

While the debate between the spouses was settled, a new conversation ensued about the etiology of that man choking in my presence. Had the choking occurred because we were talking about it? Had we attracted the negative manifestation? Or was God/Spirit attempting to teach someone to believe?

I like to think that God/Spirit uses me as needed. Whatever the case, that evening would be the last time to date that I had to perform that maneuver. It left me completely convinced that Spirit was in charge!

By the way, I still have that winter white suit…somehow, I just can't part with it!

**

And so, after saying goodbye to beloved friends and family, we headed for the west coast of Florida. Very soon after arriving I enrolled in graduate school at the University of South Florida; I would be taking counseling courses towards a Master's degree. It was there that a fellow student told me about The Center for Positive Living (CPL).

One Sunday Chip and I braved a torrential rain to attend and found a full audience. We enjoyed the teachings about positive thinking and became loyal followers of a brilliant young man who was the leader and teacher. I credit him for my continued interest in the subject of Manifesting and The Law of Attraction.

We decided to take a class on Manifestation. One of our first assignments in our beginner's class at CPL was to manifest something other than a parking space…though we did that also. I had decided that the reason we were finding parking spaces up front was because most people did not bother to seek them so close. I was a healthy skeptic yet , and needed something more measurable in order to be convinced.

I chose a very small growth on my back, believing it

would be a worthy challenge to have it heal and fall off. I set my goal for that to happen, put it in writing and then, frankly, forgot all about it. One day as I was drying off from a shower, I looked down and there it was…the growth had fallen on the floor! It had healed. I was so blown away…so excited…like a child that had discovered a jar of cookies! Wow! I am going to have fun with this process called manifestation, I thought.

Now I was ready to set another challenge. I had what a hand surgeon diagnosed as arthritis in my left thumb. I did not think it was arthritis as I had no other signs but this small bump on the thumb. It was quite painful at times.

I set a goal to have it disappear. I would constantly massage it. I knew that I would know when to go back to the surgeon…it took a year of massaging it many times daily in a circular motion. One day I got the message…go see the doctor and have it removed. So, I returned to the hand surgeon. He took an x-ray and said you have a small neuroma…a growth on the nerve in your thumb. "I will easily remove that."

I was thrilled! I would now have proof to show my class that manifestation worked! I requested my x-ray of the arthritic thumb.

"I never told you it was arthritis," the surgeon said.

"Oh, yes…look at my chart and the old x-ray," I replied.

"I can't because they are tied up in the legal system because I am breaking up a group partnership and going into solo practice."

I so wanted those two x-rays.

Spirit then said to me, YOU know it happened, you don't have to prove it.

I agreed, but still it would have been nice to see it on the film and read my medical records. I wanted the x-rays to show the class that manifesting was powerful!

The growth was soon removed in an outpatient procedure and officially diagnoses as a neuroma. I think I had irritated it so much it attached to the nerve in my thumb.

So that was my introduction to conscious manifesting something I wanted to happen in my life.

Since words begin with thoughts…one must monitor one's thoughts very, very closely.

How often I would catch myself making a negative affirmation…it is something that bears WATCHING AND MONITORING ALWAYS!

One of my favorite songs, written in 1944 by Johnny Mercer, seems to sum it all up:

Ac-cent-chu-ate the positive,

E-lim-mi-nate the negative,

Latch on to the affirmative,

Don't mess with Mister In-Between!

"Just when you think you have your life all mapped out, things happen that shape your destiny in ways you might never even have imagined. The coincidences or little miracles that happen every day of your life are hints that the universe has much bigger plans for you than you ever dreamed of for yourself."

~Dr. Deepak Chopra

Chapter Eight

MANIFESTING MANY MANSIONS

*M*y life was a happy one. I had met the man who would become my husband for forty years. I was deeply loved by him and my heart returned that love for all our days together. As the saying goes, "Life begins at forty," and for me that was true.

As I delved deeper into the art of manifesting, I realized that I had been doing it unconsciously for much of my life. I just didn't have a name for it. Now that I did, I was surprised to find that my strong belief that good things were happening to us was apparent in my everyday life. I was becoming aware that when I truly believed something was going to happen or the right person, place, or thing would show up, it usually did!

The first home that my husband purchased was my first conscious actions of manifesting something of a physical nature. We were in the throes of our courtship. I was divorced and he was separated and waiting for his own long drawn -out divorce to be finalized. We already knew we would marry in the future.

It was a chilly evening and we were entertaining another couple at my home for dinner. As I bent down to light the fireplace I felt a feeling like a butterfly fluttering its wings and flying out of my heart. That is the only way I can explain it.

When I told Chip about the butterfly, he chuckled and said, "Well, I will keep an eye out for it. What time are Bob and Gay coming?"

I glanced up at the clock and said "Now!" It was six o'clock and soon after the doorbell rang. I did not give the odd sensation in my chest another thought.

The next morning the phone rang; it was Chip, telling me that his step-mother had died the evening before. The person who called to give him the news said they had found her sitting up reading the newspaper and, as far as they could determine, the time of death was about six p.m.! Was that the butterfly I felt leaving my heart? As soon as I asked myself this question I got goosebumps up and down my arms.

Chip also informed me he would be flying to Georgia the next day to settle the estate. His father had left him their little home by the stream, in which he grew up. Apparently, he already had a cash offer for it.

Wow! I thought, *You are just perfect, God!* It was a modest home, but it would bring enough for Chip to buy himself a home in the next town. He no longer had to wait for his divorce to go through.

Little did we know how perfect the timing really was. Months later we learned that his step-mother had an appointment with an attorney, the morning after she died, to change the deed and leave my husband's childhood home to his ex-wife! The two had had a close relationship for over eighteen years.

It made me think deeply. How does one explain that?

Was there a Divine Intelligence beyond what even we who are full of faith can fathom? One more day and Chip would have lost what was rightfully his.

Armed with that knowledge I decided it was time to "put it out there" to ask God to manifest what he needed for our future home. So I did just that. I had learned not to outline how things would happen. Just put the thought and words out into the Universe in a positive manner stating it as if it had already been fulfilled. Writing it seems to strengthen the affirmative prayer. I thanked Spirit/God for answered prayers in advance, show gratitude by saying thank you and the most important step of all... Let Go!

"Sometimes letting things go is an act of far greater power than defending or hanging on."

~ Eckhart Tolle

And thus, the hunt for his first home began. We learned that Chip could qualify for a mortgage below what we would need to stay in the upscale town we both lived in. So, with my Realtor friend in tow, I began to hunt in other communities south of us. I soon found, however, that these homes were also well over our budget. Divorce is very costly.

Suddenly my friend recalled a home that was not being shown. It was on an acre of property, on a lovely street at the crest of a very small hill. It was also constructed of brick, had a beautiful swimming pool, five bedrooms and a finished basement. The best part was, it had just been reduced by thousands of dollars

"What is wrong with it?" I asked.

"Oh, there is a huge problem. First, it is tied up in a divorce case..." Then she began to laugh. "There is a large dog tied to the post in the basement that no one is taking out for walks so he has to use the floor as a place to do his business—and he has diarrhea!!!—which is why no one will show it." She wrinkled her nose in disgust. "The smell is just awful!"

I am a nurse and a mother of five children. Nothing, certainly not a little dog diarrhea, was going to stop me from seeing this home. I looked, I liked it and made the top offer we could afford, though it was well under their asking price. Two days later it was accepted. It seems the divorce mediation stipulated that they would accept any reasonable offer.

Wow! It was my first awareness that manifestations could happen quickly. Chip got busy hiring professional cleaning companies and laying tile himself in the kitchen to make a home for his future bride.

After two years there, I wanted to go back to our old town. It was a closer commute to work for both of us and they had a better school system. My husband was not very happy, but after a few discussions he agreed... with two conditions. I had to find a place with no grass and no pool. We had spent two years caring for an acre of grass plus a large pool and he didn't want to deal with it anymore.

I had become a Licensed Real Estate Agent and was up for the challenge. I had our home appraised and was not surprised to find that it would sell for a huge profit. I was also not surprised to know that it was still at the low end of the price range in our former town.

I made a conscious decision to call in my angels, God, Spirit and Mother Mary and say an affirmative prayer. I thanked God in advance for finding me a home. Most importantly, I believed that it was possible—this is known as "lining up vibrationally" to your affirmation.

I had also learned that when manifesting, letting go of your desire is THE most crucial step. I believed it showed that one had faith in the process.

I now needed to wait for the home with no lawn, no pool, and within a certain price range to appear.

When I announced the parameters to the sales force at the real estate company where I was employed to be on the outlook for such a property, they laughed out loud.

I didn't let their reaction discourage me. Instead, I practiced the mental balancing act that manifestation requires.

Each day, as I went about tending to my family and my new busy profession, I kept an eye out for a home that fit my specifications, all the while reminding myself that mani-festations often take a long time.

The homes I was seeing were highly priced, and all had immaculately manicured lawns; most had lovely pools as well. So, I let go and let Spirit do the manifestation. I KNEW it was going to happen someday.

"Someday" turned out to be much sooner than I thought!

One day, as I was driving down the main road in town, I heard an inner voice say, "Turn into that driveway!" It would not be the first nor last time I made a turn based on some other worldly advice. Driving down the long driveway, I soon spotted a lovely two-story home with a circular drive in front. It was painted blue-gray with white shutters and crisp white double doors, and had a front porch with square white columns. It looked like a modern day, contemporary version of a Southern style mansion.

Yet, unbelievably, this stately home that was carved out of three acres of tree filled land, had NO GRASS AND NO POOL! I loved it at first sight, and was sure my southern husband would also. I got out of the car and went up the extra-wide brick-edged stairs and saw a lockbox on it. It was for sale! I looked for the name of the Realtor on the lockbox and it was the one I worked for! What? How did I not know about this listing?" Bursting with excitement, I quickly entered the home.

The floor plan was a contemporary play on a center hall colonial, with a large living room and dining room to the left and a sunken family room off to the right. This room was truly lovely, with a unique large fireplace with a post as a mantle that matched the paneling on the walls. The hearth was made of a beautiful stone. It even had a bay window!

Upstairs there were four bedrooms, including a master suite with huge walk-in closets. I spent the next few minutes hurriedly checking out the three bathrooms, laundry room and oversized garage, then I ran back to the car.

On the way back to the office I had to remind myself to stay within the speed limit; I couldn't believe what I had seen. When I got there I sought out Bryan, the owner/broker and asked him who owned the house that was obviously new and not finished inside.

"Oh, it just went on the market this morning," he replied, "I sold a builder friend of mine a very large piece of land for the building of dozens of homes, and he wants to get rid of the single home where he has considerable capital tied up."

I felt the goose bumps rise up on my skin and knew it was a sign that something was about to happen, something connected with my affirmative prayer. Perhaps it was God's way of answering me?

I did not know the builder, but I called him and set up a meeting. His name was Michael, the same name as one of my sons, which I considered a good start. After my experience of finding my husband's first home, I was sure this was the answer to my prayer. I did not know exactly how it would happen, but that was okay—one should not outline - Spirit/Angels/God would take care of the details.

Before Mike appeared, I looked for the listing but it was not even out yet. Suddenly he came in the office door and said to me, "Hey, why don't you buy my home so I can get on with the building of my new development?"

The funny thing is, this very gregarious man did not know I was interested in the house; he spoke to me because I happened to be the Realtor on call and was sitting at the desk up front.

"Just look at this beauty..." he said as he handed me a copy of the listing that would appear in the next day's multiple listing service," It's going to be gone by tomorrow."

Not if I can help it, I thought, then I looked at the price and my heart sank. It was double the price of our first home and way out of our reach. Well, I decided if Spirit had found this home for me there should be a way to afford it. I would just have to listen and learn.

By now Bryan had joined us, and I told them that I wanted to buy the home but needed to bring the price down. I also would have to sell my home, which in my humble opinion would sell quickly.

Then Bryan said, "Well you know you don't have to pay a commission because I give a one-time waiver of the commission to my associates."

"WHAT?" I said incredulously, "No, I did not know that!"

In an instant, the price had dropped by thousands of dollars! That wasn't enough, though; I needed to reduce it by another fifteen thousand dollars. Where would I find the rest? I brazenly decided to write up a contract and present it right there to the builder; I would offer him the price we needed to buy it for and stipulate that the deal would be contingent upon the sale of our home. I quickly prepared the contract, put in the offer and let it go.

When I got home I told Chip what I had done.

"Good Luck!" he said, with a good-natured chuckle, then added, "But I should never say it will not happen with you 'doing your thing'!"

I did not hear anything from the builder for a couple of days but I barely had time to notice, for suddenly our office got very busy. It seemed everyone wanted to sell and/or buy a home! So I was shocked when Mike suddenly appeared in the office, walked up to my desk, threw a signed contract onto it and said, "We've got a deal! It's yours!"

I was floored! Tears flooded my eyes as I thanked him.

Later, Brian explained to me that in order for Mike to proceed with his new building he had to free up the considerable cash he had tied up in that piece of property. But there was even more to the story. It seemed there was a small problem with the home...or, more accurately, with people's thinking. . All the Realtors in the area thought it was built at the wrong end of town! In fact, everyone had been telling Mike that, which was undoubtedly a factor in his decision to sell so quickly.

Little did they know that within a few years the prices at that end of town would skyrocket, after an interstate highway was built nearby with an exit to our location in town.

I was looking to the future possibilities for that area. There were several lovely office buildings lining the neighboring access road, which hinted at the development to come, and in fact Chip's office would move there before we moved into the house! And that was just the beginning. I had not only manifested our perfect home, but an excellent investment property!

Our current home also sold quickly, to one of the first people who saw it and for the listing price. In the meantime, Mike found out I had been an interior decorator before going into real estate and he asked me to guide him in choosing the interior finishing touches of our future home. I was having fun picking out my cabinets, countertops, and flooring, all with no money down... another miracle manifested!

Awestruck and more than a little bit curious about my new "power," Chip began to talk to me about the principles of manifesting. He was very methodical, carefully researching the subject online and printing his findings for me. I just giggled to myself, for I really did not care to know the details of the process...I just knew it worked for me!

After twenty-five glorious years in our three-acre wooded paradise, it was time to do some more real estate manifesting —specifically, a buyer for our beautiful home and a home in Florida to live in when we retired. I decided to "put it out there" and, to be on the safe side, I also began to do a small vision board of the kind of home we wanted in Florida. I envisioned buying a small ranch and started to cut out pictures of palm trees, us riding on our boat, all the good stuff!

Vision boards are fun and great for identifying broadly what you do want to manifest.

The many Florida Keys had been our favorite winter vacation spots. Rental prices were always sky high during the winter , but we were both working and could afford it. Now it was one year before our planned retirement, and I cajoled Chip into looking at some homes on the mainland around the Keys. It wasn't convenient to live on the Key itself, as we would have to leave it just to get groceries; we were also concerned about future building and traffic. A home on the mainland with access to the Gulf of Mexico for our boating seemed to be our best choice.

One day we were riding around looking at areas when I spotted a sign that read *Buy Your Boat a Home.* It was an open house sign in a community that also had a large marina. That would just be perfect, I thought, as Chip turned into the development and stopped at the Open House. I jumped out of the car almost before he pulled to a stop.

A pleasant man in his eighties answered the door. He quickly introduced himself as Frank, then announced, "The realtor's not here but I can sell my home myself."

I knew that to be true if it was in his contract, which Frank showed me.

"Ching…ching…ching…" went my mental calculator as I motioned to Chip to follow me into the home. If Frank did sell to us directly it would take thousands off the asking price! Then I saw what the asking price was, and my heart sank. For though it was dramatically less than our current home it was still more than we wanted to invest as we wanted no mortgage. This was based on a five-year retirement plan we had drawn up at age fifty.

Faced with this fact, I silently called on my angels, Spirit and God. Suddenly, the homeowner said "You know, I have all the money in the world but no buyer…and I have to be out of here by Easter."

"That's funny," I quipped, "we don't have all the money in the world but we sure would like to be in a home by Easter!"

We all laughed at that one.

"I really like this home!" I added, truthfully and with enthusiasm. Next to me, I could feel Chip looking at me as if I had two heads. My belief in manifesting our own reality had become so strong that I knew that this home was going to become ours.

There was just a small problem: most of our money was tied up in the equity of our home up north. By now it had more than doubled in price and I thought it would sell quickly. We weren't planning to put it on the market until after our daughter's wedding, and that was in six months. To buy this Florida home, Frank and his wife, Molly—whom we had yet to meet—would have to sell us their home for practically no down payment until we got the proceeds from the sale of our northern home.

Frank once again astounded me by saying, "Can you give me five thousand dollars to hold it for you?"

Just five thousand dollars?! Somehow, I managed to stay calm.

"Sure," I said, "If you make the contract contingent upon the sale of our home."

"Oh, that's no problem. You will just have to send me the listing. Is it in a nice town? How much will it sell for?"

He knew the upscale town we lived in as it was the head-quarters of a Fortune Five Hundred company. Chip was employed there in a high management position. That seemed enough information for him.

Satisfied with our answers, Frank said, "Let me go get my wife!" Then he darted to a back room and returned a moment later accompanied by a silver-haired woman with a soft voice and a suspicious expression.

"Molly," Frank said, "These kids (we were fifty-four years old!) want to buy the house!" Though his voice was deep and commanding, he was smiling like a Cheshire cat.

Molly was not smiling...in fact, she did not look the least bit happy. She proceeded to ask us about the details of our home up north.

He kept interrupting her with statements like, "I will throw in all the kitchen dishes and stuff";

"I will help you in any way I can!";

"I will throw in the tools in the garage,"; and, repeatedly,

"Don't worry! I have the money!"

By that time, I had a few years of experience in Real Estate as a Broker and was not too shy about negotiating.

It was clear Frank was the decision maker and he wanted to "get rid of this Florida house and boat."

"Will you give us a mortgage?" I hopefully asked. After all, he said he had lots of money.

"Sure, I will! How much do you need?"

I gulped and said, "But wait, *you have not heard my offer yet!*"

"Oh that's right," he said as if brushing off a minor detail, "What is it?"

With another gulp I gave him my number, which was *fifty thousand dollars* lower than his asking price. . We were still about twenty-five thousand dollars apart. Molly was looking at me like I was crazy, or maybe like I was trying to pull a fast one. I ignored her stare and continued.

"I will give you the five thousand dollars if you will take back a mortgage for no interest. As soon as the house sells…which it will quickly, I will give you the balance in cash." I said all this as fast as I could.

Upon hearing my offer Frank summoned Molly into the other room for a conference. She must have objected to the sale, because Frank exclaimed,

"We have so much money…these kids need our help!"

I kept sending pink, the color of love, to them and visualized the house being our home.

Sure enough, when they returned to the living room, Frank bellowed, "You have a deal!"

I almost fell over flat on my back! Before he could change his mind, I said, "Look, I'm a real estate broker (I had attained that status years earlier) and I can write up a contract for you."

In all the excitement I had spotted contracts on his desk. "You can take it to your attorney and he can review it as to the terms, with the exception of the sale price and the contingency of the sale of our home …how about that?"

He readily agreed, and after I wrote up the contract Chip and I headed off to our rental home on the Key. We had just bought a home for five thousand dollars!

"You are a piece of work," Chip said, shaking his head in disbelief. "Now, Ms. Manifestation, how are you going to sell our house quickly when Amy wants to stay there for her wedding and you promised her she could?"

"Oh, I will think about that later," I replied. "Let's go for a walk on the beach and find some shells!"

Soon the call came to pick up the contracts, which had been approved by Frank's attorney. This came as no surprise; given how fond of us he seemed to have become. I thought Frank would have fired his attorney if he had not approved it.

Chip and I transferred the required funds and just like

that we owned a home in Florida.

When our vacation ended, I got down to the business of selling our home. We wanted to put the house on the market in early June, and hopefully set a closing date in September, after Amy's wedding. So much to do! It also seemed unreal that we now owned a home waiting for us in Florida. We had not heard a word from Frank.

The showing of our home was very slow...hardly anyone but Realtors and their associates looked at it. I think it was because we had a closing date at the end of September. Most people wanted to be in their homes before Labor Day, so they could be settled in time for the new school year to begin. That meant we had to attract a buyer who did not require a school.

One day, I was sitting on the brick patio reading when a truck pulled into the circular driveway. A young man wearing a blue uniform with an ad on the pocket climbed out. When I asked how I could help him, he explained that he and his wife had just lost a baby and she wanted to move somewhere private in this town. The house had to have hardwood floors, he added. He looked like the least likely person to purchase our home but the inner voice said, "Don't judge a book by its cover" as clearly as if I had a radio on.

I was particularly taken aback by his remark about the floors. Just the day before a dear Realtor friend had come to see the house. She suggested that I take up the carpet in the large living room and dining room. We did so right then and there and threw all that carpet in the basement. Underneath the dark carpet were gleaming finished hardwood floors. She also suggested I take down the heavy draperies and put up sheers to lighten the rooms. *Hmmm...* I thought as I listened to the young man, *That was no accident!* It was Spirit at work!

He introduced himself as Max and said he knew my three older children from high school. That put him in his early thirties. *Wow!* I thought, my wheels turning, *He must be very successful to be able to afford this home.*

He spent about twenty minutes in our home, then thanked me and left. The next day Bryan called me.

"You have a full price bid coming in on your home tomorrow!"

"What? Is it someone named Max?" I asked, though I already knew the answer.

"Yep...that's the name," Bryan replied.

I wanted to scream to Max, *Put the offer in now because someone else might over bid you!*

It wasn't just for me; after hearing about the loss of their baby I wanted them to have our home.

I shall never forget that phone call. It was the Sunday morning before we entered the official contract on our home. We were watching Dr. Schuller's Hour of Power on TV. I just had time to tell Chip about the contract on our home he had yet to sign when the phone rang. It was Frank, the seller and mortgage holder of our Florida home!

"I was wondering if you could pay off your mortgage soon? I need the money," he asked rather abruptly. I was astounded that this call came in literally the day after the offer on our home. I remained very calm but was thinking, *this is amazing!*

"Sure, I think we can do something...but that's a lot of money. Could you discount it by five thousand dollars if I pay it off this month?" I asked brazenly.

I glanced at Chip staring, incredulously, at me because of my outrageous offer!

"Oh, sure that will be no problem!" Frank said quickly.

What? Was I living in a dream world?

No, I was just manifesting what I put out there! Oh My God! I would now have an extra five thousand dollars to decorate the house in Florida!

Even now as I write this, I realize that it sounds rather naïve of me to think it would happen without a hitch and that Max's full-price offer would be signed the next day...but *that's exactly what happened!*

Frank was sent a certified check for the balance of the mortgage and we were the proud owners of a lovely home for our retirement. As I said you have to believe it is going to happen with all your mind and heart and soul...and when I want to manifest something I do believe it at the deepest level.

With the wedding now behind us we had to find a place to live until Chip's retirement at the year's end. We quickly found a three-month furnished rental, where we would stay through the Christmas holidays. As we packed up our home, we gave the kids the choice of whatever furniture, antiques, and artwork they wanted. The rest would be sold or given to charity. We then put the stuff we were taking with us into storage until we were on our way.

Chip and I arrived in Florida excited to begin our new life there. Though we fell in love with the yachting community, it was soon apparent that the home was too small for visits from our large combined family. I quickly formulated a plan to redecorate the small home, sell it and buy another, larger place in the same community.

We had sold our boat up north and purchased a larger one, I hoped that new home would be on the marina that opened onto the Intracoastal Waterway. Once again, I applied those tried and true principles: declare it, deeply believe, it would happen, give thanks, and then the hard part, let go and trust it would happen!

Manifesting our next home was truly unbelievable.

We had just returned to Florida after a vacation in Cape Cod. On the way home from the airport I saw an estate sign at the entrance of our community with arrows leading down to the water. I do love estate sales, especially in Florida, as many elderly people have dear old treasures. After the plane trip I wasn't sure whether Chip would want to go, but he indulged me.

I didn't find anything that I wanted at the estate sale, but I did see a woman sitting at a desk in the living room. When I said hello, she replied, "Do you want to buy the house? It's for sale!"

What??? It was directly across from the marina where our boat was floating with its lines securely tied. I could see it from the living room!

"What is the price?" I asked casually.

"Oh, it is priced to sell. The owner's husband, a physician/surgeon , has died and she wants to go to an assisted living facility as soon as possible."

OMG! Another case of "money is no problem", but I had to move fast! As I was experiencing a major déjà vu moment, my husband was outside on the lanai looking at the big party jacuzzi pool they had installed. It was a unique concept I had never seen before.

I quickly went through the home and found it was exquisite, with a sunken living room and an elevated dining room. It had a rather small kitchen for a house of more than three-thousand square feet, but the large family room with a built-in bar, exposed beams, lovely fireplace and sliding glass doors more than made up for it.

There was a wing with two large bedrooms and a full bath, and another wing with a huge master bedroom, oversized bath with a jacuzzi and privacy garden, and another large office overlooking the water. There was yet another bath serving the living areas. How perfect!

But the price was much too high. After we left Chip and I discussed the possibility of extending our present home and putting a pool in.

Then I said, "Why don't we put an offer in on the house? I would like to put money from savings down as a deposit and take a mortgage out until our home sells."

Chip was appalled. "That is a preposterous idea! They would never take that low an offer…it was appraised for more than that. Besides," he continued, "We decided to have no mortgages."

"It would only be a temporary bridge loan," I countered, "not a mortgage, per se. And, you never know...they might accept our offer."

And so with his blessing I contacted the listing realtor. A week went by and we heard nothing, so we began to make plans to enlarge our home. I distinctly remember Chip showing me sketches of a pool and a second floor for more bedrooms and a bath ....and that's when the phone rang.

"This is Laurie, the listing realtor," a voice said, "Mrs. K. has accepted your offer." HOLY COW! This news blew even my mind! It was an offer that was nearly *one-hundred thousand dollars* below the listing price! I told her that my husband and I needed to talk and I would call her back. When I told Chip he chuckled and said, "You figure it out, Ms. Realtor." By now he was used to these magical things happening to me.

Now what do we do? I asked myself. I certainly did not want to draw from our investments. The first thing would be to put the house on the market, above our purchase price. Then I would look for a position in the nursing profession.

I ran out and bought a newspaper and right there in the classifieds was the perfect job: a new psychiatric unit for women was opening and they needed a charge nurse. With a R.N. and a B.A. in Psychology, twelve credits toward my master's degree in psychology, plus my psychiatric nursing experience, I was sure the job was mine.

That was Sunday. When I called to answer the ad the next morning, they scheduled an interview for that day!

I was excited as I listened to them tell me about the

unique, eclectic program that included not only traditional counselors but consultants in art, dance and psychodrama.

There was even a corporate piece of outdoor equipment used for trust walks high up into the sky.

Within an hour of my interview, my phone rang. I was hired!

This was Monday...just twenty hours after our offer on the water-front home was accepted.

I called Laurie back and agreed to go through with the signing of the contract on the water-front home. Needless to say, we listed our home for sale the next day.

The nursing position I planned on getting would turn out to be a dream. It paid well and miraculously it was five days a week—no weekends!

More importantly, I was doing what I loved most—helping people. I worked with women, most of whom came from middle and upper-class homes, who had been diagnosed with depression; many had been battered by their husbands.

I learned that there were many forms of battering women; some of them passive. Very common was the verbal abuse. This knowledge would become invaluable to me in the future. Though I was new to this particular field I soon became adept at counseling the members each morning at the nine a.m. unit meeting.

Meanwhile, home sales had slowed down, and though we were asking the lowest price at which one could buy into the marina community, it remained on the market for months. I never panicked, though, because I knew that Spirit had sent me a Charge nursing position that would not only help others but help me. Besides that, I had money to play with over and above paying the bridge loan. Sure enough, one day a couple came along and offered us full price with an immediate cash closing.

Though our plans for the house were working out, I decided I had no intention of leaving my nursing position. I would stay there until the unit was closed by the insurance company because we were not giving enough medication and our patients were getting well!

In the meantime, I had extra money to completely re-decorate the big house. There was white everywhere; flocked white wallpaper in every room, white double draperies with sheer underneath and white carpet. The interior decorator in me was having a field day bringing color and warmth to this beautiful home. It was also so joyous to cross the street to our boat and sit on it to read. I was simply in heaven here on earth.

Chip, on the other hand, was not a happy camper. He felt the house was far too large—there were eighty-two steps, he pointed out, from the master bedroom to the refrigerator! I told him I would buy him a mini-refrigerator for the bedroom, but that would not suffice. We sat down and had a conver-sation about the pluses and minuses of owning the house—a process we call "Ben Franklining it."

Aside from the size, he found the waterfront too noisy. The fishermen arrived each morning at four a.m. and the sheriffs who housed their boats in our marina arrived at six, and Chip heard it all. It didn't both me, though, as I left for work at six-thirty.

I pointed out that there was a very significant upside—the house had appreciated far above what we paid for it. In addition to my love for—my home, the realtor in me desperately wanted to hold onto it as an investment. However, Chip's dislike of this house was so strong that I eventually agreed to put it up for sale. If my husband was not happy no amount of money could override that.

Just as sunshine enters your life so do clouds appear. As my eldest daughter is fond of saying, "Life spins on a dime!" How true that was. During a routine physical, the young physician said to Chip, "Hey, they have a new blood test called a PSA that is good for picking up early cancer of the prostate. Want me to order a test for you with your bloodwork?"

It was an afterthought, asked very casually, and Chip replied, "Sure. Can't hurt to check, especially since my father had it."

We never gave it another thought, until the nurse called to tell us the physician wanted to review the bloodwork with Chip. We both knew this meant trouble was brewing somewhere. Sure enough, at the appointment the doctor informed Chip that he had a very aggressive prostatic cancer. Because he was so young he would need radical surgery. We left the office that day shocked and upset—Chip had never even been in the hospital before!—but we were grateful that it was operable.

Immediately, we got down to business, scheduling the surgery for as soon as possible and pulling the house off the market so we could focus on his health. Thankfully, Chip tolerated the surgery very well and was home in a few days.

Once he had recovered, we agreed it was time to relist the house for sale. It pained me to do it—I was in love with the home and the location; I had also warmed it up considerably with my decorating. The all-white was gone, as were the heavy draperies. The heavy front doors had been replaced with etched glass doors with sand hill cranes that showed the stunning water view of the harbor and the marina. I had often fantasized about more modifications so it would be even more lovely

I also knew that these waterfront homes would skyrocket in value, one day selling for millions. Yet money could not be a consideration; Chip was very unhappy in the house; in fact, I believe he would have died had we stayed.

Purchasing a new home, however, presented a bit of a challenge. We had paid the mortgage off as soon as we sold our previous home, and between that and our other investments we did not have a lot of ready cash. It was time to get serious, which for me meant calling upon my Angels to help me manifest a buyer and a house for us to purchase.

In the meantime, I began to prepare our home for sale, and this was what I was doing on the evening the phone rang. It was about a week after we had decided to relist the house, but—it's important to note—we had not yet done so.

"Hello," said the male voice on the other end, "I am a real estate agent and I know your home is off the market, but I was wondering if there is any way you would consider selling it? I have a buyer who is desperate right now. He moved here from Asia and was supposed to close on a home in your community." He then told me the sale had fallen through because the sellers could not get a mortgage on their new home and the sale was contingent upon that. "My client's furniture is on the moving truck. There is only one thing he must have—a living room wall that is at least sixteen feet long."

Is this for real? I thought. *Can it be that I am manifesting a buyer before the house is even listed?*

"Well," I said, quickly putting on my broker's hat, "I do have the living room wall he needs. We can let you show the home with the understanding that if they buy it the commission would be three percent—not six or seven percent—because there is no listing realtor."

"Oh, that's fine," he quickly replied, "Would five o'clock tomorrow evening be okay with you?"

I agreed that would be fine and we said our goodbyes. Then I went to tell my astonished husband.

Just before five the next evening, Chip and I each grabbed a book and a bottle of water and walked across to our boat. From this vantage point we could observe them but they would not see us. Soon the car pulled up and the Realtor got out with two people in tow. They entered the home and left about ten minutes later.

"Well, that was the fastest visit I have ever seen," I said to Chip, "Let's go back and get ready for dinner."

The phone rang that evening about eight o'clock. It was the Realtor, asking if he could come over and present an offer!

"Of course," I responded nonchalantly, thinking, *Oh well, they are probably going to lowball us.* After all, they had been in and out of the house so quickly! I even considered the possibility that they were investors wishing to flip the house.

About fifteen minutes later the door chimes rang. I opened it to find an elderly gentleman standing there, business card in hand. He gave it to me, and when I looked down I could not believe my eyes—his first name was the town I was born in (which, by the way, was most unusual), and his last name was the maiden name of a dear friend who was a female physician.

Was that a strong sign? Had I manifested a buyer this quickly? I thought so because I had that tickly feeling that comes when this magic begins. Without a word to Chip, I invited the Realtor to come in.

"Well, this is going to be quick. I have a full price cash offer with the closing date in three weeks!" he said confidently.

"What?" I exclaimed. The house was over 3000 square feet and moving from it would be a major undertaking.

He explained that our living room wall could accommodate the buyers' sixteen-foot oriental panels; that was all they really wanted. That was really synchronous, as during my first marriage I'd had four lovely oriental silk panels adorning my living room. We sold them when we decided to move, but they were among my favorite pieces of art.

"Well," I said, stunned, "this is a surprise."

I then asked him if Chip and I could have a few moments to speak privately. I wanted to be sure he was up to the move. Chip readily agreed to take the offer and worry about where we would buy later.

A worst-case scenario would be to put the furniture in storage and rent for a short while. And so, we signed the contract, which had already been signed by the buyers, then said goodbye to the Realtor and rejoiced. We had increased our house-buying budget considerably and would look now for a desired Gulf-front home. Again, my mind was just blown by this manifestation! What was the next purchase going to be? I felt that I was truly living in a fantasy world.

We searched high and low and soon discovered there was a downside to living on the Gulf-front on a public beach, even one that was rated one of the loveliest in the world. For one, the prices were sky-high, even for a one-bedroom condo with no storage space. The beach was also noisy in the evening and early morning.

During our search we were invited for cocktails at sunset and were nearly blinded. The owners had a dark blind to drop down during the day to help with their exorbitant summer air conditioning bill.

Chip and I didn't give up easily, but after a sale-by-owner with a friend also turned out to be a dead-end, I realized that my dream of living Gulf-front was dashed. As we drove home, I was unusually quiet and fighting back tears.

Though I was very disappointed, my logical side soon kicked in. It didn't make sense to sacrifice a large space for a view. It was not worth the exorbitant prices when we could be just a bicycle ride away from the beach in a newer community with a larger home than a condo.

All of these things were going through my head as we neared home. There were two entrances to our community, and though we lived closer to the front entrance Chip decided that day to go in the back-entrance. That is when we saw the **Open House - For Sale by Owner** sign. This was unusual; open houses were frowned upon in our community and when they did happen it was on a Sunday. Today was a Tuesday.

We stopped to see the Open House and a young blonde woman in a bikini came to the door.

"HI!" she exclaimed, "Come on in...I was just sunning myself."

It was March and a bit cool out of the sun, yet the fans in every room were going as well as on the lanai.

As I stepped inside I drew back at an unpleasant, very distinct odor. It was dog poop, mixed with cat litter! I chuckled to myself as I recalled the first home we bought and the dog with diarrhea.

Were my angels sending me a message? If so, they certainly had a sense of humor! As I stood there and tried not to breathe through my nose, I began to suspect that Chip and I had found our next home.

Sliding glass doors opened from the living and dining areas as well as the family room and master suite; unveiling a vista of blooming shrubs and flowers in pinks, yellows, and hues of purple, some nested in a beautiful butterfly garden.

The garden surrounded the oversized pool with a plethora of glorious flowering hibiscus and flaming scarlet and white bougainvillea bushes were nearby.

There were mango, banana and avocado as well as lemon and orange trees. I felt I was in Paradise!

I also spotted a very large ferocious looking black dog—the source of the odor—tethered to a pole.

A gagging sound brought me back to reality and I glanced over to see Chip putting his hands to his throat. He was also looking at me like I had lost my mind. Though the child in me was giggling, the adult realized that we had to address the issue of the dog poop odor and whether it could be removed.

In the meantime, the woman was chatting away about her husband to another couple. He was a security consultant who helped young people—usually from wealthy families—who had been arrested in foreign countries. It was the husband's job to negotiate their freedom. Apparently, his work carried certain risks as well. He informed us that he had permission to carry a concealed weapon, which he did at all times. Not fond of guns at all I really was a bit taken back.

He explained then that the dog, upon his command, would leap for the neck and jugular vein of anyone and hold on until he was told otherwise. I glanced back at the dog by the pool and had no doubt that his owner was telling the truth.

He then nonchalantly pointed out the heavy metal guard screening on the bottom half of the lanai; this too, was necessary for passersbys. They had cats as well, and as he and his wife both had busy work schedules, they provided potted palms around the pool for the cats to use as litter boxes; the dog used a small patch of grass on the one side of the pool. No wonder it smelled!

Intrigued, I wanted to hear more, but one look at Chip and I knew I had to get a move-on. He couldn't stay there much longer and I hadn't even seen the rest of the house yet. I gave him a thumbs-up sign and quickly scurried around the place, noting that all it really needed were cosmetic changes. The colors were loud and different in every room, from orange to yellow, bright green and blue, and the floors, though one-half-inch solid oak, were dark and badly stained.

On the other hand, the master bedroom was large, with a huge walk-in closet and a bathroom that had a separate shower, double sinks, and a large, deep corner Jacuzzi, which, as a bath person, I considered a big plus.

The other wing held two large bedrooms with a bath in between. Attached to the side of the house was a large greenhouse that I could air condition and open up to the rest of the house and use as my office. It was perfect.

The pool was in need of new paint and a cleaning but it was oversized and was surrounded by the over-sized screened in lanai.

We were told that botanists lived there previously, which explained the green house and the plethora of lovely flowers, blooming bushes and fruit-bearing trees.

The roof and air conditioning units were fairly new and there were hurricane shutters and an oversized two-car garage with lots of cabinets and a work bench area. There was also a good-sized laundry room with a closet.

I completed my tour with visions of decorating dancing in my head, only to find that my husband had escaped to the car. After telling the owner I'd be back in two hours, I dashed out after Chip. My work was cut out for me, I knew, but my husband had always trusted my real estate instincts. I crossed my fingers, told my angels to surround me with the light, and went to face the music!

As I left a British couple were standing in the hallway, arguing about whether to make an offer on the house. The wife wanted to, but the husband was dragging his heels.

"Let me think it overnight, please, darling," he said in his clipped tones.

It was a warning that I must act quickly. The sellers were anxious to close as soon as possible. I decided that when I returned that evening I was going to make an offer. First, though, I had to convince my husband.

For the next hour or so, I pled my case. Chip already knew my capabilities as a decorator, as I had earned a living doing that. Now I reminded him of the dog with the diarrhea in the first home he purchased and how easily commercial companies could remedy the problem. I pointed out that the dark floors could be refinished and white-washed for a delightful Florida look. Removing the clashing colors on the walls would do wonders to update the house. As I spoke I found myself becoming more and more excited by the challenges this house presented.

I then got serious, stating it was my belief that the out of control dog was a sign from the angels that this crazy manifestation process was at play. I even teased him by saying, "Remember, dog is God spelled backwards!"

When I was finished, Chip gave me an exasperated look. "What are you going to do, Bobbi? Buy this house for a dollar?"

Though we had a contract on our home, our cash would

still be tied up until the closing. Chip was conservative in all ways, especially when it came to finances. He did not believe in mortgages when retired.

"Yes, I will sell it for a dollar!" I replied very exasperated. For crying out loud, how many times must I show this man that the angels or the Universe or something magical was guiding us? Did I need to remind him that I had manifested a salesperson whose name was so significant in my life?

Besides, we weren't completely "retired"; I was still working full-time and he was teaching college classes in the evening. We had lots of extra income.

Finally, Chip relented. "Okay, as long as you are willing to risk it."

There would be no financial risk at all because I would make the house contingent upon the closing of our home!

"You really think that anyone is going to sign a contract like that?" he asked incredulously. "Yes, I think they will because he knows the value of our home here on the water. I will tell him it is an all cash deal!"

The next miracle, and one of the most outstanding examples of synchronicity in my life, to date, happened that evening when we returned to speak to the owners.

As we walked in, taking care to breathe through our mouths, I was so sure this was to be our next home. We exchanged pleasantries and then sat down to negotiate the terms of the contract I had written up. Before long we had agreed upon a price, which was in itself a miracle. Nowhere in this prestigious community could you ever buy a home of that size for the amount we offered.

The other terms I proposed were equally preposterous. I asked that I be able to send in a commercial cleaner and a painter *before* the closing! I also wanted the carpeting in the bedrooms taken up and the underflooring scrubbed.

"And what if you don't close?" the seller asked.

"Well then," I replied, "I will put new carpet in your bedrooms and you will have yourself a newly decorated home and you can raise your asking price!"

It made sense to me. But honestly, I felt like someone was leading me and even telling me how to respond.

Once everything had been settled, I pulled out my checkbook.

"What are you doing?" the seller asked.

When I told him I was going to give him a five-thousand-dollar down payment to be held in escrow, he replied, ***"Just write the check for a dollar."***

Chills ran up and down my spine and my husband just looked at me and shook his head in disbelief. And so we all signed the contract and went out for a Dungeness crab dinner.

Even though I laughed in delight, it blew my mind that the Universe, Spirit, God, would know that Chip challenged me to purchase this house for a dollar! Even after so many manifestations, I never ceased to be amazed at these perfect outcomes. I also never stopped asking, *How does this work? How is this happening?*

Who and what had caused this person to say something my husband had said hours earlier? I did not believe in an anthropomorphic God. But my mind was spinning! What forces are at work in this Universe that are yet untapped? How do our minds transmit spoken words to another? What is this thing that I am calling Miracles or Magic? These and other questions would lead me to study the brain and quantum physics that I continue to do today.

Now it was the time to get to work. After hiring a few commercial cleaners and a painter and flooring company that smelly, "one-dollar" house was transformed into a lovely Florida home. I had such pleasure viewing the changes I had envisioned on the walk-through, including replacing the greenhouse with a large Florida room with oversized windows overlooking our lush landscaping.

Even after all these years, I get chills every time I remember that man saying, "Just give me a dollar"! We would spend twenty glorious years in that home.

Cozy Cottage

When first I saw this little place
It was an unspeakable filthy disgrace
Then I looked beneath the dirt
And soon realized how you must hurt
Built long ago with care and love
By those who labored with a glove
What happened to you is quite sad
For long ago you were quite the "pad"
No one recently has cared for you
Not even added a classic color or two
Viewed again with a different eye
Revealed the beauty within that lie
All that's required is a loving touch
Scrubbing, painting, flowers and such
Walls and floors-showing beauty each morn
When the handsome hues will adorn
Bringing joy to those that made me new
And a heavenly haven I will promise you.

Chapter Nine

MANIFESTING A MEDICAL MYSTERY

*L*ife was joyous in our new home. We loved the pool, especially when our children and grand-children came to visit. We spent hours and hours boating with our wonderful group of friends and enjoyed many vacations, visiting all but four states in the U.S. and many countries around the world. We also took a couple of dozen cruises. Life was wonderful!

Our trip to the Canadian Rockies was particularly memorable. It was the end of June, and Chip and I were enjoying the break from the Florida heat. One beautiful, crisp summer day, we had just finished a lovely visit to the Butchart Gardens in British Victoria and were looking forward to heading over to Lake Louise, where we had accommodations.

Neither of us had never ever been to this part of Canada and we were basking in the breathtaking scenery. As we traveled up the Trans-Canadian Highway I marveled at the steep cliffs on the right-hand side of the road and the regal rising mountains on the left. There was also little to no traffic, as we planned this trip a week before the 4th of July.

Suddenly, I heard what sounded like the roar of a train on the passenger side of the car. I also thought I heard sounds of hoofs, but surely there could not be anything coming up that steep cliff! How wrong I was! We pulled over on the shoulder of the road and spotted three female mountain goats or rams…we were not sure. They were followed by an enormous male with a huge rack of antlers, who was rapidly nearing the car. He was going to protect his harem. He very cockily sauntered up to the window, coming within a half-inch of it, and peered at us intently. He was intimidating, to say the least!

Trying to lighten the moment, my husband quipped, "He is looking at you, not at me!"

An amateur nature photographer, Chip had his camera at the ready within seconds. I, on the other hand, felt a bit afraid. What would happen next? Would he begin to ram the car glass? We had both heard cautionary tales of the elk in Banff walking down the streets, but there was nothing in the literature about dealing with a huge, aggressive mountain goat.

After what seemed to be a long time, but was really only about five minutes, he turned on his heel and very slowly walked away. Clearly, his body language was sending the message, "I own this place, not you, and I will get out of the way of your car when I feel like it!"

We soon got back on the highway, but I was left uneasy. I could swear by the way the mountain goat had looked into my eyes that he was trying to tell me something.

My mood began to lift as we distanced ourselves from the animal and chatted about the impending birth of our granddaughter, who was due on the Fourth. A little while later we stopped to photograph a waterfall, completely en-grossed in the beauty before us. The mountain goat incident was all but forgotten.

Our destination, Lake Louise, was about a ten-hour drive away, so we decided to stop overnight in Kamloops. After a good night's sleep we would have breakfast, then continue to the rustic lodge we had reserved.

As we arrived we began to see the snowflakes slowly falling. We hadn't seen snow in years, and to watch the flakes floating down to grace the branches of the tall, elegant evergreen trees was like a dream! I had hoped for snow and said as much to my beautician, who had spent the early part of his life in Canada.

"It never snows there in July," he'd said, "Don't even bother with scarves and gloves."

But I knew better. Before our trip I had done my own research and discovered that there was a slim possibility of snow in July. I also practiced my Law of Attraction, visualizing what I wanted to see, then letting go of the outcome while still holding the picture in my mind's eye.

Now, I stood there in the mountains of Canada, marveling at the beautiful pastoral picture I had envisioned. I put on the gloves, boots and scarf I had packed and went outside and started to make angels in the snow! I was like a child frolicking and when my husband joined me we had a snowball fight! What a blast!

That evening the phone rang and we learned of the birth of our granddaughter, Julie. Mom and baby were doing just fine and we spent several euphoric minutes talking to our daughter about this latest addition to our family.

I was so busy rejoicing that I never gave the goats

another thought. But later, as I slipped into bed and gave thanks and gratitude for our newborn granddaughter and many other blessings, the image of the large male mountain goat suddenly appeared before me. I grinned and said nighty night and went to sleep.

The rest of our trip was so wondrous as to defy description; there was, however, one small disappointment. The snowstorm had closed down some of the higher elevation roads so we could not go on our planned two-day mountain trip. Instead, we happily enjoyed the majesty of Lake Louise and the arrogance of the huge elk walking down the main street and golf course in the city of Banff.

On our way home, I felt a bit tired. Chip headed to one of the parks with his camera, hoping to spot an eagle. I wanted to go but found I just could not summon the energy. Though this was highly unusual I didn't give it much thought as I sunk into the lovely large jacuzzi at the motel.

Chip came back in a couple of hours, full of excitement; he had spotted an eagle and took a picture of it. It was the perfect ending to one of the top five most memorable vacations I'd ever experienced.

Upon reaching home, though, I was feeling very tired. So much so that I laid in bed watching a morning news show. Suddenly my vision went dark and a spiraling, black vortex appeared before me. I had to quickly get to the bathroom for it felt like all my body contents were emptying. I did not know what was wrong, but I had warning bells ringing in my mind.

It was then I remembered discussing the mountain goat

incident online with a nurse from Hawaii. She was very much into "signs" and metaphysics. She told me that the mountain goat—or ram, as she called it—was a warning sign that something was wrong with my head! At the time, I dismissed it as ridiculous folklore. Now, while in the grips of this mysterious ailment, the ram once again appeared in my mind's eye, sending shivers all over my body and causing the hair on my arms to stand on end.

It was enough to call my doctor, a rare occurrence. Instead, I utilized many complementary therapies such as acupuncture, craniosacral therapy and regular massage; I also ate well and took vitamins and minerals. I was a high energy person who enjoyed wellness. Now, though, I felt in my gut that something was really wrong with me.

When I called the office, Ruth, the doctor's nurse whom I knew well, said, "Bobbi, don't come here. It sounds like you need to go to the ER at once."

Chip was in the other bathroom shaving when I announced that I had called an ambulance. "What is wrong, Bobbi?" he exclaimed as he rushed out, "What is the matter?"

He was tearful and shaky as I replied calmly, "I have something very wrong with me. I don't know what it is but I just had an incident of tunnel vision, a blackening of my sight...in fact I think I fainted while I was lying down!"

Minutes later, I was in the ambulance, en route to the same hospital where Chip served as a Chaplain, his second career. Once in the ER I was hooked up to a monitor that checked my vital signs, then blood was drawn and other samples taken.

The physician on duty and a male RN tended to my evaluation. After about two hours the nurse walked in and said in a cold, crisp manner, "There is nothing wrong with you; all your vital signs are normal, as is your blood work. I would suggest you are under stress and perhaps would want to see a therapist or a counselor."

There it was again—the "hysterical woman syndrome" females have suffered from since the days of Sigmund Freud! But *I knew* something was wrong with me, and the ram kept manifesting in my mind's eye.

At this point Chip was becoming irritated with me, as was the doctor, who kept insisting I was going to be discharged.

I am very, very slow to anger, but when the male nurse announced, "I am writing your d/c order right now," I became furious! *Why did they never listen to the patient?*

"I am not leaving," I said loudly and brusquely, "and I am going to hold you legally responsible if anything happens to me! I am a Registered Nurse with advanced degrees and certifications. I rarely go to a doctor and I have never been to this ER."

Even as I write this I can picture the doctor looking at me with his arms folded across his chest.

"So, you want the million-dollar work up?" he said mockingly.

"Yes," I replied curtly, "I am worth it!"

"Okay," he said, adopting an almost threatening tone, "I am going to order an MRI!"

I did not answer him, nor did I speak to my husband, who by now was completely embarrassed by his defiant wife.

Within minutes my gurney was sliding toward the radiology department. They saw me very quickly and I soon was back in the ER, where I felt the staff was looking at me in a not-too-friendly way. Exhausted, I dozed off to sleep, only to be awakened by the screeching sound of the curtain being drawn around me. I opened my eyes to see Chip standing over my bed; there were tears in his eyes.

"They are going to admit you," he said.

"Good!" I said, thinking of the old days when they admitted you to the hospital for further testing.

The doctor appeared a second later, with his arrogant stance and haughty tone.

"You have a growth in your brain." he said very coldly, "It is either an abscess -"

I cut him off. "Don't be stupid! My white count is normal, my sed rate* is normal and I am not febrile*."

He ignored me and continued, "Well the growth is…"

I spoke right on top of his words, as if we were singing a duet. "…either malignant or benign. "Thank you, doctor. You are fired! Get out of here and leave me alone!"

Turning to Chip, I asked him to call Megan, the Director of Nurses, and a dear friend. She quickly came to the ER and spoke with me, then gave us the name of the neurosurgeon

---

* Erythrocyte sedimentation rate (or "sed rate") is a blood test that shows inflammation in the body.
* feverish

that, as I requested, "is the one you would trust with your mother's life."

After receiving Chip's call, Dr. Souler arrived quickly. He was so compassionate and brilliantly competent. I instantly trusted him with my life as well.

I felt a sense of relief and peace that the MRI had shown the tumor, and I was filled with gratitude for that technology. At no time did I entertain the idea that the tumor was malignant, nor at any time was I apprehensive or frightened.

However, I did ponder the ram and his possible involvement in this. Could it really be, as my friend suggested, that the animal was part of the complex plot and was sent to warn me? If so, how was that possible? What is it that we don't know? These questions spun through my mind even as the drama swirled around me.

My husband called our adult children, some of whom were vacationing in the Outer Banks of North Carolina. He then called my twin brother, who wanted me to fly to Boston for the neurosurgery. This was not surprising; we from the Northeast believed it was the very best city for medical treatment.

When I mentioned this to Dr. Souler, he said, "Tell your brother I was the Chief Resident of the large Boston teaching hospital that he wants you to go to, and I am also the U.S. representative for a company who trains neurosurgeons to perform complex neurosurgical procedures with the computer software they manufacture."

Hearing this, my brother—and my husband—were both assured that I was in good hands.

As a nurse, I was focused more on the technology involved in the procedure. I was actually going to be operated on by a computer-guided device, with the surgeon looking not at my brain, but at a screen. How fascinating!

I asked Dr. Souler to show me the equipment in the OR and he promised he would. He was not amenable, however, to my suggestion that I stay awake as they removed my skull and the tumor, something I knew they did in China. Though the brain lacks nerve endings and I wouldn't feel any pain, Souler denied my request. That was a bit disappointing to me but I trusted that he knew best.

There was also the very real concern of seizures while on the operating table. They debated keeping me in the hospital for a period before the surgery, but when I promised to take my anti-seizure meds faithfully they decided to let me go home for a few days.

On the morning of the surgery we arrived at the hospital around five a.m. While pre-medicated and heading into the operating room, I said the prayer that called for protection from The Blessed Mother Mary. Though at this point she had not visited me in many years, she had always remained in my prayers.

"Mother Mary," I prayed, "please show yourself to me in some way. Let me know you have not forgotten me, who loves you so much." Suddenly, the potential seriousness of my condition crept into my consciousness. *What if it is not benign?* I thought. "Keep me safe and watch over me. Thank you, Blessed Mother. Amen."

Even in my hazy state, I recalled how as a young woman

fresh out of nursing school I worked in the OR. I loved my service there. The OR team was a closed, select group with a camaraderie all of its own. Doctors and nurses were on a first-name basis and we thought of ourselves as family, apart from other hospital personnel. We had a lot of fun despite the seriousness and often sad cases that were presented for surgery. I often think our healthy sense of humor protected us from the horrendous things we saw and prevented us from crying behind our masks.

As I lay there on the stretcher, waiting to be placed on the operating table, I wondered what the environment in this OR would be like. When I told the nurses I had been an OR nurse they immediately high-fived me! There was still that bond.

They all assured me everything was going to be fine and that I had the most handsome anesthesiologist in the world. "Wait until you see his blue eyes!" they said, one after another, which struck me as funny as I was now in my sixties and a grandmother. I couldn't have cared less what the anesthesiologist looked like; I just wanted him to know that my veins were easily collapsed and that for this long procedure he needed to go into a major vein in my neck or he would lose me on the table.

That said, I certainly couldn't argue with the nurses' assessment. The first thing I noticed when the anesthesiologist walked in was the incredible blue eyes over his mask. We began to talk and I asked him where he was from.

"Wayne, New Jersey," he replied.

As a New Jersey native, I knew Wayne very well. "Where in Wayne?"

"Well actually, it is in a small town close to Little Falls…"

I gasped. Little Falls was where I had graduated high school.

It was then that the Blessed Mother Mary appeared, hovering high on the left side of the operating room. I saw the glimmer of what I thought was a small smile on her face.

"What street?" I asked the doctor."

"Riverside Circle."

"WHAT!? That is incredible!"

I told him that one of my older brother's best friends had lived on that street. In fact, my son, who was sitting out in the waiting room, was nicknamed for that friend. When I gave him the family name, the doctor said "Yep…they lived right next door to us."

"Oh, Mother Mary, you are so perfectly divine," I said, and she responded "Put that in your next book." She then faded from view.

I am NOT going to write another book, I thought, *just let me get out of here with a brain that functions one hundred percent!*

Knowing it would be futile to talk about this manifestation to the surgical team, I said nothing about Mother Mary for fear that they would think I was hallucinating and give me a harmful drug.

True to his word, Dr. Souler came in and explained the workings of the computer while "Dr. Blue Eyes" administered the IV. My last thoughts before I drifted off to sleep were how far technology had come since I worked in the OR and how grateful I was for those advancements.

The next thing I knew I was being pushed out of the recovery room on a stretcher. I saw the faces of my husband, my son and a dear nurse friend who had come to sit with them. With great effort, I summoned all my strength and raised my thumb to them, then promptly went to sleep again.

I awoke to the sounds of "I'd Rather Be a Hammer Than A Nail" and I chuckled. It was one of "our songs" played during our courtship and sung gleefully by us. More importantly, it was the song that was played after my NDE ! And so the synchronicity…the magic… lives on!

The good news was brought in by my loving husband— the tumor was benign! We hugged each other and I told him to leave and get some rest! I then had time to think.

What were the odds of having an anesthesiologist who grew up in that small town in New Jersey, thousands of miles from where we were now? What were the odds that he would be the next-door neighbor of my older brother's close friend, the same friend my son was nicknamed for?

Do you see why I have to believe in manifesting…in the Connectivity of All Things? In the Divinity of Mother Mary? In the Power of Prayer? In God, Spirit or a Higher Being who, no matter what you call it, is somehow weaving our lives together? To me it seems magical!

This cannot be scientifically explained! Although many who read these accounts will discount them in some way, there are now too many people reporting these events for our scientists to ignore the Power of Prayer and the role of a

Divine Being. They need only look at quantum physics to see how it is laid out for us.

Divinity Revealed

She appeared to me once again, this time in Blue
Did she know I called on her to see me through?
Another crisis in my life; though this one small
She was always there for me...for them all!
What will the sign be she will send this day?
I don't know...I just continued to pray.
"Affirm everything will be alright," she said
As on the Operating Room table I was led
It was then that she showed a miracle to me
The anesthesiologist and I grew up to be
From the same town- thousands of miles away
I knew then that she held me in her arms that day.

Chapter Ten

MANIFESTING THE DRAGONFLY

"I can still only see a dragonfly, its wings as thin and light as silk and its body the color of a rainbow. But on the wings of this dragonfly I take off and fly, for my soul carries no weight. It is our bodies – these borrowed vehicles of flesh and bone – that weigh us down. Our spirits are eternally free and invincible." ~ Daniela I. Norris

I don't know why, but I have always been fascinated by dragonflies. I see them as one of God's perfect creations and even have art, jewelry and pottery with dragonfly themes. Little did I know that this beautiful spiritual symbol would appear in my life as a strong sign of synchronicity, and another divine miracle.

Shortly after moving to Florida Chip and I had started attending church. Though not completely fulfilled by its teachings, I'd always found serenity when singing in a church choir; it brought me peace, and put me in touch with my divinity. One of the first people we met there was Cindy, one of the church's chaplains. This warm, friendly woman made us feel welcome at the church; she also formed an immediate bond with Chip, who was serving as a hospital chaplain.

On our first meeting I noticed Cindy wore an exquisite diamond dragonfly pin. When I complimented her on it, she replied, "Someday I will tell you the significance of it."

Cindy's husband Chad was a retired professional baseball player whom my daughter Allison, a fanatical Yankee base-ball fan, had identified as a Most Valuable Player (MVP) from decades earlier. I didn't know Chad that well, though he quickly proved himself to be a very personable guy with a wonderful sense of humor and a generous spirit.

It was Christmastime, and Chip and I were participating in the church's annual pageant. That night, the choir lined up for the processional in our white robes with golden metal wings; halos adorned our heads. The plan was for us to walk in singing the Christmas carol, *We Three Kings of Orient Are.* Chad, who was a very tall, large man, was dressed as one of the kings. His crown kept falling off, and his amusing comments had us all laughing out loud during this solemn moment. I thought Cindy and Chad were a wonderful couple that complemented each other perfectly.

Months later, Cindy would tell me about their son Jim. He was one of their blended family of nine children. Jim was in his early thirties when he died of cancer, leaving behind two children, including a nine-year-old son. Throughout Jim's illness Cindy had provided support to her grandson, answer-ing his questions and doing her best to comfort him. The best way she had found to explain his father's death was by telling the Story of the Dragonfly, which she also shared with me.

Once, in a little pond, in the muddy water under the lily pads, there lived a little water beetle in a community of water beetles.

They lived a simple and comfortable life in the pond with few disturbances and interruptions.

Once in a while, sadness would come to the community when one of the fellow beetles would climb the stem of a lily pad and would never be seen again.

They knew when this happened; their friend was dead, gone forever.

Then, one day, one little water beetle felt an irresistible urge to climb up that stem.

However, he was determined that he would not leave forever. He would come back and tell his friends what he had found at the top.

When he reached the top and climbed out of the water onto the surface of the lily pad, he was so tired, and the sun felt so warm, that he decided he must take a nap.

As he slept, his body changed and when he woke up, he had turned into a beautiful blue-tailed dragonfly with broad wings and a slender body designed for flying.
So, fly he did!

*As he soared he saw the beauty of a whole new world
and a superior way of life than he had ever known.*

*Then he remembered his beetle friends and how they
thought that he was dead.*

*He wanted to go back to tell them that he was
now more alive*

*than he had ever been before. His life had been
fulfilled rather than ended.*

*But his new body would not let him go down
into the water.*

He could not get back to tell his friends the good news.

*Then he understood that his friend's time would come
when they would know what he now knew.*

*So, he raised his wings and flew off into
his joyous new life!*

~Anonymous

Cindy told her young grandson that like the beetle in the story, his father had not died; he had simply gone on to a joyous new life with God in Heaven. Jim wanted to come back to tell them all not to be sad, that his pain and suffering were over, but he was not able. They would see for themselves one day, when they were all reunited in Heaven.

That story seemed to relieve the boy's anxiety about his father, for he asked Cindy to read it over and over again. On the day of Jim's memorial service Chad had presented Cindy with the diamond dragonfly pin. Since then she had worn it almost every day.

One beautiful fall Sunday, we arrived at church to learn some very sad news. Cindy had awakened that morning to find that Chad had passed away. The congregation sat there, shocked and saddened by the minister's announcement. It seemed impossible that such a bright light had been exting-uished so suddenly.

Later, Cindy told me Chad had complained of his back hurting—as he often did—and went into his office to sleep in his large comfortable lounge chair. When she walked in the next morning, he had already left for Heaven.

At his memorial the following Sunday, we gathered outdoors on the beautiful church grounds. Many people spoke that day about how much Chad had added to their lives. I talked about how he had so generously given my children signed baseballs and that we would all remember him as our "king."

Chad's former teammates were there as well, many of them in tears. As one of them spoke, we saw what appeared to be a very small swallow circling overhead. Round and round it went, then the lone bird came closer, circling over Cindy's head. That's when we realized it was not a bird at all, but a very large dragonfly!

I was in awe of the divine sign that we interpreted was

from Chad! We all knew it meant he was in a wonderful place and was communicating that to his family and friends, especially his wife.

How was this possible, I wondered as I watched the lovely blue dragonfly hovered above my friend's head. What *was the process that caused or allowed this to happen?* My curiosity about the subject of synchronicity was exponentially heightened after this event. To me it was magical!

After Chad transitioned, Chip had immediately emailed our daughter Allison, the huge Yankee fan with the news. Allison responded with a link to her Yankee blog, where she had posted a glowing tribute to him. She also reminded us that she had his signed shirt draped over a sofa in her "Yankee" office and his autographed ball encased. I had won the shirt in a raffle at the church fair.

"Coincidentally," Allison was due to fly down to see us – her first visit to Florida in three years. She would be flying in from Philadelphia—a first for her. As her time of arrival neared, I asked my husband to check on the pool temperature to make sure it was warm enough.

Suddenly I heard him call out to me, "Bobbi, come here…look at this!"

I rushed outside and found him kneeling at the edge of the pool. I looked down and saw the largest dragonfly I had ever seen! I can still remember the way the hair on my arms stood on end and the chills ran up and down my spine.

How had this beautiful creature gotten into our pool area? It was completely caged with screening and had doors that were screened and locked. It was a metaphysical mystery…a God thing!

Was it the same dragonfly that was at the Memorial Service? No, Chip and I agreed that the other one was much larger and was blue.

"It's a message from Chad to Allison!" I said quickly, "I know it!" And with that I got the God bumps as I was now calling them again and chills ran up and down my left side. This was something I was told was a sign of confirmation of a spiritual event. Since I could not answer the *hows?* I took it on Faith. However, that was not the end of the story.

When Allison arrived, she told me that while sitting in the airport lounge, a man next to her had said, "Wow! I think that's 'Goose' sitting over there!" When she looked over, she couldn't believe her eyes.

"Mom, you remember Goose, the retired Yankee baseball player!"

I confessed I did not know him, but now I was getting goose bumps about "Goose," big time!

Allison said he was one of fifty retired Yankees to attend the 58th Old Timer's Day on July 10th. It was the last one they would hold in the "House that Ruth built;" It was also the last one Chad would attend.

She then proceeded to tell me that she had seen the other Yankees returning from Chad's Memorial Service. I listened in stunned silence, thinking, *The divine synchronicity…the magic had continued!*

When I showed her the dragonfly, Allison immediately pointed to the sky and said in her cool, understated way,

"Thank you, Chad."

Our visit passed far too quickly, and as Allison prepared to leave for the airport, she brought out the dragonfly from the bedroom, carrying it carefully on the paper and said, "This is supposed to be given to Cindy. I just know that is what Chad wanted." We respected her wishes.

The next Sunday morning after the service, I told Cindy about finding the dragonfly and asked her if she wanted it.

"Absolutely," she replied tearfully.

I went out to the car and retrieved the black velvet box in which I had placed the dragonfly.

"That is incredible!" she exclaimed, tears filling her eyes again, then she hugged me in gratitude and sorrow. The circle of synchronicity was complete. We all knew that Chad had reached "Home Plate" and was "safe."

I couldn't stop thinking about the miraculous event, or the dragonfly's role in it. When I researched the creature, I learned that the dragonfly dates back over one-hundred-fifty million years. This ancient creature appears in many spectrums of color in their transparent, luminous colored wings. There are over six hundred types. During their first two years they are in the water. They are called nymphs and shed over a dozen skins. When they climb from the water they transform into a winged insect that has great flight capabilities. Thus, they are thought to be *symbols of transformation.*

The dragonfly reminds us that all transitions in life follow steps and that change or transformation happens over a period of time. Also, the multifaceted eyes of a dragonfly are able to see from many angles. This shows us that anything can be viewed from different perspectives, including the illusions of life. Dragonflies remind us to take flight, moving out of the stories and drama that lives within us. They remind us that we can look beyond the illusions and find greater clarity with our emotions and introspective self.

It seemed the more research I did, the more questions I had. Yes, I now understood the quanta, knew about the connectivity of all things, had a deep Faith, believed in the unseen side of life, had an open mind about manifestations, the law of attraction, BUT:

How did the dragonfly get into my caged pool?

What manifested it there?

Who/what knew I collected dragonfly objects?

Who sent the dragonfly to encircle the family during the memorial service?

What made my daughter, an avid Yankee fan, plan a vacation to Florida before Chad's passing?

What made her fly out of Philadelphia, when she never did before or since to allow her to see the Yankee players who had attended the service?

Thinking about all these unanswered questions only made me more inquisitive; made me read more; and thus, I am sure, resulted in my attracting more manifestations!

I just did not know the details of the process!

Transformation

Oh, little nymph who does reside
Beneath the soil - deep inside
A hole so often mired in mud
Many will fall back with a thud
Others cannot dare to believe
A journey's change they can weave
You believed and so you jumped
Even though you were often bumped
Others looked - seeing nothing above
But you kept on because you love
You did not know what was ahead
Still you persisted without the dread
Of the unknowns that often reside
In many - though buried deep inside
SUDDENLY! Another elevation to play
And so you continued day after day
Spreading your wings - you did not die
But became a beautiful dragonfly
Now you soar gracefully to and fro
A model of change and transformation for all
Because you always got up after the fall.

Chapter Eleven

MANIFESTING A DIAGNOSIS

I received an e-mail from my niece Nancy, telling me that her daughter Grace had been taken to a Boston hospital because of a severe headache and fever. The doctors suspected meningitis and everyone, including Nancy and her husband, had to wear protective masks around Grace. Upon reading the e-mail I phoned to learn that Grace was now at home and was doing fairly well, though she still had a fever.

As she described her symptoms and we spoke about possible diagnosis thoughts of various ailments went spinning through my mind. When I thought of Lyme disease my arms began to get goosebumps. When I mentioned it to Nan, she assured me Grace had been tested for Lyme and Strep and both had come back negative. I felt very uneasy about this, as I was getting confirmation that it was Lyme disease, yet I did not want to say anything, as both Nancy and her husband were in medical fields.

Talk turned to a graduation party and other family happenings, but as our conversation wound down I again asked Nancy if Grace had been tested for Lyme disease. Though she was adamant, I remained skeptical.

Two friends of mine had permanent damage because their Lyme disease was not diagnosed in time. In fact, missed or misdiagnoses of Lyme Disease are all too common, despite the fact that there are 30,000 new cases of Lyme disease reported each year. I was also getting those telltale goose-bumps running down my left arm. I was *sure* Grace had Lyme disease.

I told her a story about Jane, another friend of mine from Los Angeles, who had been tested for Lyme disease. Though the blood tests were negative, she continued having symptoms of the disease and was sure she had it.

She had read about a physician in San Francisco who advocated multiple blood tests be taken for Lyme, as the spirochetes did not spread evenly in the bloodstream, but "clumped." Jane knew intuitively that she must go to him and persuaded her husband to drive the four hundred miles for an appointment. She had multiple blood tests over many hours, and only *one* tested positive for Lyme disease. I was hoping Nan would relay that story to Grace's physician.

That evening I was praying for a number of people in the family: a grandson soon to be born, another grandson with challenges, and yet another awaiting a donor for a bone marrow stem cell transplant; I was also praying for Grace.

I sent brilliant white healing light to all concerned. During the prayer for Grace, a bull's eyes lesion commonly seen on Lyme patients appeared in my mind's eye. I sent the brilliant white light to that lesion and prayed Grace's parents would discover such a lesion if it existed.

Around ten the next morning I had the urge to call Nancy but decided against it. She was busy enough taking care of a sick daughter, and besides, I had often been ridiculed by family members for my gift of precognition. That afternoon I received the following email from Nancy:

"I brought Grace back to the doctor today. Almost a week into it and she woke up this morning with a 101 fever, headache, fatigue. The doc did the exam, tested for strep and was going to retest for Lyme. While we were waiting for the strep test to come back her arm started to show this huge red/purple ring. Honestly, it just appeared. She was sitting up on the exam table and I was sitting in a chair across from her and I saw it. It was huge and hot to the touch. I brought it to the doctor's attention. There is no way we could have missed it before with all of these exams she's had. It was as if God was saying, LOOK, the answer is right before your eyes. The doctor was floored. He was amazed how it showed up while we were in his office. He called another doctor in to see it to add it to their case studies. He found two more spots on her abdomen. Lyme bull's-eye!

Nan also sent me pictures of the bull's eye!

There it was—my validation! I thanked God for sending the gift of not just one large bull's-eye but several, so they would not be missed!

Like all my other manifestations, I had more questions than answers. Had I manifested the bull's eyes on Grace's behalf, or had I somehow sent the thought to her so she could manifest it? Had Nancy said, "Aunt Bobbi thinks you have Lyme disease?" Was the thought, held by me, that Grace definitely had Lyme's disease have anything to do with it? Did Grace believe in her Aunt Bobbi's intuitive abilities enough to manifest the bull's eye?

"It's often been said that "seeing is believing", but in many cases, the reverse is also true.

Believing results in seeing. "

~ Donald L. Hicks

I am happy to report that Grace recovered after a course of antibiotics and is now being scouted by colleges for volleyball scholarships. She is an awesome athlete, an inspiring leader of her team and has a delightful sense of humor. Most of all, she has an engaging yet humble personality. And—however it happened—I am so grateful that she had the capability of manifesting those bull's eyes!

Chapter Twelve

MANIFESTING A MEDICAL MIRACLE

"*M*om," my son Andy said joyfully over the phone, "you're going to be a grandmother again!"

"What?" I cried out, stunned. This newest addition to the family would truly be a miracle. Their other sons were ten and thirteen years old. Andy's beautiful wife Stephanie had health problems that had once brought her close to death and resulted in a permanent colostomy. Although we did not discuss the issue, it was clear that not having the baby had never entered their minds.

Once the initial shock wore off, I was filled with delight. It had been nine years since one of my children had a child.

"Yep, it's going to happen this spring," Andy added with pride.

Chip and I flew to Texas to be present at the birth. When I first gazed at Noah through the nursery window his physical beauty took my breath away. When I held him in my arms just an hour after his birth he looked up at me with wise eyes in a steady, even gaze that tugged at my soul.

Everyone at the nursery window thought he was a girl. As I stood there I suddenly realized that this was the same month and week that Christopher had been born nineteen years earlier. My eyes filled with tears.

Thank you, dear Blessed Mary, for the wonderful healing gift of this child. I was sure she had sent me another grandson in another springtime.

Sadly, Noah would be diagnosed with a rare immune disorder called IPEX. This would require multiple hospitalizations, regular drug treatments and eventually a bone marrow transplant. It was thought he would have a short life span but Noah was a fighter!

A few years after Noah's birth I became a chaplain at a Unity Church in my area for the period of one year. One Sunday morning, I was asked to give a short talk during the service; it was one of our tasks when the minister was on vacation. Noah was having a very tough time and he was always in my thoughts. He was also the inspiration for my words that day.

Child of God, I behold the Christ in You

Though ten years ago they had been told they could never have another child, somehow, Stephanie was pregnant. Her two sons, ages 10 and 12, would be joined in the spring by a brother.

They named him Noah, a name sent in a dream to his mother. At the age of two, he became critically ill and was admitted to Dallas Children's Hospital. He was placed in the Intensive Care Unit.

This was no ordinary ICU. This was a small, dark room, without windows. It was sparsely furnished with six little cribs. This is where the children were sent to die.

After weeks, Noah was diagnosed with Job's Syndrome, and IPEX syndrome, both genetic immune disorders. The resident physicians and pediatricians swarmed around him daily to view these rare diseases. His parents were told he probably would not live as most males only survived for one year. They said he had already surpassed their expectations.

His grandmother, a nurse, was called and she flew to Texas immediately to take the twelve-hour day shift while his mother, home with his brothers, would cover the night shift, his father would come after a long work day and stay for a couple of hours and then drive the nurse home.

Three times Noah was transferred between his private room and ICU. Most mornings there were three or four very small empty cribs. But he defied the odds three times; you see, Noah did not know he was supposed to die.

The only treatment the parents and grandmother could render was whispering gently in his ear telling him that *he would get well...he would go home.... that they loved him and so did God.* They offered prayers, asked the nurses and doctors to pray for him, gave him *Healing Touch* and sang him his favorite songs. Slowly, over many weeks, Noah got better. The doctors were amazed.

Today, Noah, though not without occasional challenges, is an optimistic, active eleven-year-old. He plays basketball, baseball, and runs track. He has been placed in advanced learning classes in fifth grade.

This is the danger of viewing anyone in a limited, subjective way. It is placing a label on a person and in your eyes, they become that label. Wouldn't our lives be richer if all people were perceived for whom they are: wonderful children of God each with the light and love of the Christ Presence within.

Noah, *who is one of my six grandsons*, thinks so… for he is truly a Child of God…whole, well, and free.

Update 2018

As he approached his teens, Noah experienced some very tough times. He could not tolerate the treatment regimen that was proscribed for keeping his immune system functioning. The symptoms simply would not allow him to attend high school. He would undergo dozens of hospitalizations and eventually had to be homeschooled. Yet he remained an outstanding student, and a computer whiz; he was also a devout Christian with a very positive personality. He often would calm his mother's apprehensions by saying, "Let's Pray about it."

No matter how tough things got, Noah's thoughts were always on getting well. Even when the blood work and his symptoms showed that he was failing to thrive and that his only chance for long term survival was to have a stem cell bone marrow transplant, he never gave up.

After visiting many medical centers from Boston to Cleveland, Noah, then sixteen, decided to stay closer to home and have the transplant done at Emory University. To their credit, Stephanie and Andy listened very carefully to Noah's input as well as the endocrinologists. It was very important that he had faith in his physicians and felt comfortable with the facility.

Noah knew all there was to know about the syndromes and his medications as well as any medical intern. He also realized the risks of the transplant; the odds were only fifty percent that it would help him. Most importantly, though, he knew his positive attitude would play a critical role in his condition.

It soon became apparent that he would have to have the procedure, and soon. Not only was he very ill; he was also nearing the outer age limit and chances of success were decreasing. In fact, if it was up to the doctors it would have been done at eight years of age. But Noah was not ready then.

As soon as Noah made his decision it was as if God went into action. The doctors immediately found a suitable marrow donor—a miracle in itself. At the same time a brilliant immunologist from a top medical facility transferred to Emory Medical Center. He would take the helm of Noah's medical team, which already included physicians of many specialties.

This lead physician was acquainted with medical research done in Italy on two brothers with the same diagnosis as Noah. They were the recipients of Extracorporeal photopheresis (ECP), a procedure used to strengthen the immune system. While the patient is under light sedation, the blood is taken out in increments and put into a clear jug. It is then spun around in a centrifuge until the white blood cells and platelets are separated from the whole blood; the cells are then chemically treated with a photosensitizing agent and subsequently irradiated with specified wavelengths of ultraviolet light before being returned to the body. The process takes three to four hours.

Usually, ECP is performed *after* the bone marrow cell transplant, but in Noah's case it would be done three times a week starting about six months *before* his transplant. The immunologist hoped this would put Noah's immune system in an optimum condition. As a nurse, I thought it was a brilliant decision and in my humble opinion would turn out to be a major factor in the success of the transplant.

When it came time to begin the ECP, I flew to Atlanta to see it for myself. It was amazing. The nurse in me looked on in awe as the doctors performed this miracle of modern science; the grandmother in me looked upon my precious Noah and prayed the procedure would help him.

Finally, the day arrived when the doctors deemed Noah strong enough to receive the stem cells. Now the question was, would they still be able to find a donor after all this time?

Little did they know that on the other side of the country, an earth angel awaited their call. His name was Adam, and he had already helped countless others with his frequent blood donations. When shortly after his eighteenth birthday he learned about a *Be The Match* registry, Adam decided to sign up. It was a chance to bring the gift of his bone marrow cells and healing to someone critically ill.

About a year after joining the registry, Adam got a call for a fourteen-year-old boy. He started the typing procedure, but was told the patient was not ready for a transplant. Another year passed he was called for the same teenager, only to learn that the patient's health status had changed and the transplant could not be done. Two years later, in 2015, he was matched with a different patient and for the third time was informed that he could not continue. Then in August he got a call about the *original* patient, who was now seventeen and finally ready for the transplant. That patient was Noah.

On the date of the donation, Adam lay in his Texas hospital bed, his proud, supportive family gathered around him. In Atlanta, Noah and the rest of our family were overwhelmed with joy and gratitude. The cells taken from Adam's bone marrow would be used to save Noah's life. They too gathered as a family and prayed for Adam with praise and thanksgiving. It would be a year before they could meet or know each other.

After all the procedures Noah had already been through, the receiving of the cells was, in his and his parents' words, rather anticlimactic. Basically, he was given a large injection containing the cells into his intravenous line; in fact, when they asked when the transplant would start, one of the nurses replied, "Oh, he's already had it!"

But Noah's journey was far from over; to reduce the risk of infection following the transplant, he would spend the next few months in isolation in the Ronald McDonald House across the street from the hospital. During this time he was very weak and often felt ill, both from the transplant and his medications; he even lost his hair. Through it all, however, he kept a positive, prayerful outlook on life, and on his medical condition.

The physicians always leveled with Noah, telling him and his parents that they hoped for the best but were not at all sure what the outcome would be. Though he appreciated their honestly, Noah held steadfast to the belief that the transplant had worked.

Slowly but surely, Noah began to respond to the cells. First his skin cleared up, followed with the lessening of the symptoms of Crohn's disease; from there, it touched every cell and organ in his body. Though he still had months of recovery ahead, it was finally beginning to look like the bone marrow transplant was a success. Now cautiously optimistic, the doctor did warn him that he may no longer be a blonde; it depended on the donor's hair color.

"I don't care," Noah replied, "I just want hair!"

The week before Christmas my eldest daughter and I flew up to Emory to be with him in the Ronald Mc Donald house. Our goal was to let his parents take a much-earned break and get away from the hospital environment and the stress they had endured for years. After we were there a couple of days the doctor informed Noah that he would be going HOME on Christmas Eve!

What a glorious celebration this holiday would be, and how appropriate for this devout young Christian to be home on the birthday of Jesus, with whom he was on first name basis. When the neighbors heard the news, they got busy secretly decorating Stephanie and Andy's home, inside and out. They even put up *two* beautiful Christmas trees!

That Christmas Eve, Noah, his nose and mouth covered with a mask, arrived home with his parents. Over the next few months he continued recovering with grace and humility. Once the doctors gave the green light, his many friends began to visit, and soon the house was constantly filled with the teenagers who had stood by him for years.

That was two years ago. Since then Noah has made remarkable strides – he graduated from high school, enrolled in a local college and got a part-time job. He has a lovely girlfriend who is also in college.

A year after he returned home, Noah was notified that *Be The Match* was holding a soiree in honor of Noah and his donor Adam. It was truly a magical evening, for though these young men and their families were meeting for the first time they all shared an incredible bond that was hard to put into words. As they chatted, Noah and his parents were shocked to learn that Adam was from a small town in Texas, *the same city where both Noah and Adam had been born!*

Talk about synchronicity! It truly was like magic! Again, who, what, how was this arranged? What are the odds of them both being from the same small town in Texas?

Though Noah was already a strong believer, it was yet another blessing for him to realize just how closely he had been held in the arms of God. After all, who but God could have arranged that?

A Divine Gift

So unique a child was he
He prayed when he was only three
Always peaceful, patient and kind
With an inquiring, curious, gentle mind.
When things went awry- as they often do
He would say, "Let me pray with you,"
And leaving one feeling so serene
An extraordinary boy though barely a teen
A wise old soul was sent - one we knew
Was one of God's special chosen few.

An Act Of Love

He was but a young lad of seventeen
A loving personality-with eyes so keen
He was aware that others were in need
And wanted to help them with a good deed

He was often called by his heart to give
His precious blood so another would live.
What inspired him at this young age
To give of himself like a wise old sage?

One day he saw another call to donate
Stem Cells needed- he could hardly wait
Another chance to give to others to live
And so his bone marrow he would give
To an unknown young man so critically ill
And Life once again in him he would instill.

Chapter Thirteen

MANIFESTING A PEACEFUL TRANSITION

*C*hip and I had spent forty glorious years together, twenty-five of them spent in our beloved Florida, where we enjoyed temperate winters and abundant flora all year round. It was a marriage filled with diverse interests, many friends, lots of hard work, family challenges, deaths, births, love, joy, sorrow, and vacations that we had always dreamed of. To put it simply, we had a wonderful romance.

As I look back, trying to recreate the beginning of our final goodbye, I realize that it began years before our physical separation. We were sitting in the opera and I noticed the program in Chip's hand was shaking. I asked if he was okay.

"Yes," he replied, "I'm fine … just a bit chilly."

The wife in me wanted to accept that answer, but the nurse in me was on full alert and insisted on a visit to a neurologist. He diagnosed Chip with Essential Tremors and ordered a medication. Thanking God it was not Parkinson's disease we went on to enjoy decades full of life, love and travel to the Caribbean, Europe, Canada and forty-six states.

Then one day, quite out of the blue, Chip arrived home out of breath. "I got disoriented," he gasped, close to tears, "and could not find my way home."

He then mentioned a familiar street—and a main artery—very close to our home.

"You are safely home now," I said as I hugged him, "It's okay."

Even as I tried to reassure him, I was churning inside as I thought of all the possible causes of this cognitive lapse. I checked his vitals and did a cursory neurological check on him, but he seemed fine. I then called his neurologist and got an appointment for the next day. Maybe, they told me, he was just overheated and dehydrated from playing golf. Still, I couldn't shake the feeling that something was happening to his neurological system, something that could not be detected.

The doctor disagreed. She found no changes in Chip's condition; in fact, he passed every test she gave him with flying colors.

"His cognitive skills are superb!" she said to me. She did, however, increase his medication for tremors to twice a day. Life continued as before, and though I observed him closely I saw no further signs or symptoms.

It happened again one morning. Shortly after he woke Chip was talking to me and could not say the noun in his sentence. "I can remember it," he told me, "but I cannot say it."

Though I managed to hide it, the nurse in me was filled with alarm. Instead, I simply provided the noun he was looking for.

"Yes, that's it!" Chip said, and he continued on with his story.

I, however, couldn't ignore the red flags. I called the neurologist, who told me to bring him right in. At that appointment, she confirmed what I already knew: Chip had aphasia. It was a special kind, she told us, he would not be able to say nouns though he could remember the word. This, she added, would be progressive and affect other parts of speech eventually. Other than that, all his tests were normal. That was a huge diagnosis though she took it lightly. Did she realize how it would impact his life? or mine? Try talking without the use of nouns. It is almost impossible.

Although the doctor was a bright, well-educated young woman, I was not satisfied with her diagnosis. I wanted to delve deeper and see if there was an answer—some type of therapy or medication—for this specific type of aphasia.

I phoned a personal friend who was a pediatrician and asked her if she knew of any memory specialists. She responded immediately, telling me that her younger sister, who was only in her fifties, was having cognitive difficulties as well and undergoing tests with a brilliant PhD. who specialized in memory testing. I quickly made an appointment for Chip.

The day of the test he was whistling cheerfully, even as he complained about the length—six rigorous hours with an hour break for lunch. When he returned later that day he said with much difficulty, "I aced the tests."

A week later, as we sat down in the doctor's office to await the results, Chip was his usual affable self. He was looking forward to getting it over with and having lunch at one of our favorite gulf front restaurants. I, on the other hand, was apprehensive; I knew something was wrong.

When the doctor reviewed each test, it did not sound too bad; in fact, I thought the results of his memory test were very good for his age. However, whenever the doctor used the word *average* my husband bristled.

"Average?" he asked incredulously, "I am a member of Mensa! I have never been called average in my life."

Admittedly, I was a bit taken aback by Chip's arrogant-sounding response, for it was completely out of character. When he was a young executive, he and a friend took the Mensa test on a lark, just to see if they could pass. Chip had, but he never attended meetings nor spoke of the society; he also never, until that day, referred to his extraordinarily high IQ.

Ironically, he would be diagnosed with Pick's Disease, a rare form of dementia that is prone to attack those of high IQ. It felt like some sort of cosmic, and very tragic, joke.

The man I married was full of integrity and honesty. He lived a service-oriented life and had a cheerful, positive disposition, along with a Georgia accent that made him sound a little bit country. Indeed, he possessed a razor-sharp intellect, but he also had a loving heart and a kind, generous spirit.

Recently, though, his personality had slowly begun to change. He had also, in the course of about a year, completely lost his facility with nouns. Then, ever so slowly, his cognitive skills began to slip. Driving the car one day he took a left turn on a red arrow! I was petrified, and when he did it again, I realized that he was having major, rapid changes.

With a heavy heart, I called the DMV and arranged for them to assess his driving skills. As she spoke with him, the woman at the DMV realized he could not legally drive any longer. That was a huge blow to Chip, as he loved to drive and enjoyed his cars. I was even more upset when I saw how furious he became. He was also irrational—blaming women everywhere because his physicians were females, as were the employees of the DMV that day—which was completely out of character for him.

It also became apparent that he could no longer handle the finances, a task he had always enjoyed. This man, who had an MBA in accounting was now unable to subtract two-digit numbers. After he double paid several bills, I reluctantly admitted it was time for me to assume control. I worried how Chip would take this, but he was actually relieved. I, on the other hand, faced a steep learning curve. Thank God I had studied accounting in college and had kept up with our financial plans.

As I slowly became accustomed to using Quicken and the spreadsheet on the computer, I tried to keep him in the loop of what I was paying. However, it soon became apparent he did not understand, nor did he care.

After decades of sharing the business of life with a partner, I suddenly found myself taking care of most things by myself. I can do this, I told myself, and I gave it my level best. Before long, though, it became clear that running a large home and keeping my eyes on Chip became too much for me. As much as I hated to leave the place where we had been so happy, I knew it was time. But where would we go? I began putting out positive affirmations and expressing gratitude in advance that we would be led to the right and perfect home.

As I awakened one morning, a thought came to me. Very

dear friends of ours lived in a gated community I had always liked. It was lovely and bustling with activities; most importantly, it was safe and maintenance free. I had broached the idea of living there, but Chip thought the community's villas and homes looked too much alike. He was interested in a more upscale community and a private dwelling. Though I wanted to make him happy, I knew, given the way his condition was deteriorating, that this was not the path to follow. I called the on-site Realtor and scheduled a tour.

I don't know whether it was his illness or just a change of heart, but as we checked out the community Chip couldn't have cared less about the sameness or size of the villas. Instead, he was like a young child, running to the banks of the ponds to look with delight at the fish, ducks and even an alligator! He also saw Sandhill Cranes and Ibis birds. He loved it. As for me, I was ready to down size and to shed my maintenance responsibilities. Chip and I had spent many countless weekends and vacations in a thirty-five-foot RV and a thirty-two-foot boat cabin, so sharing small quarters were not a challenge.

When the tour was finished, the Realtor told us to come back when we had a contract on our home and we would see what was available for sale. Thanks to a very slow real estate market the house would not sell quickly, however when we did receive an offer it was a decent one. Even after decades of synchronicities I was still surprised to discover that our buyers lived in a small town in Georgia ... *the same town where Chip had been born!* It was also the birthplace of his parents, and his uncle had served as president of the local bank!

What were the odds of that happening? And there was more—the buyers were also professors at the same small college from which Chip's dear aunt had graduated.

Clearly, we were getting very strong messages from Spirit that these were the right and perfect buyers. And so, though the price settled upon was less than we were asking, we agreed to sell our home. Now it was time to manifest another place to live.

When I reached out to the onsite Realtor at the community he had some disappointing news: there was very little for sale and none were the model I had chosen.

But that could not be so! If Spirit was arranging all this I *knew* our villa was there. I began to pray and affirm it so. I envisioned our new home and the water and the birds we would see out the sliding glass doors in the living room.

So I made an appointment anyway. The Realtor showed us two small villas and other very large homes on a pond – homes I loved but were too large.

I arrived back at the office, disappointed but undeterred. I said, "I know something will be coming on the market soon." I was that sure of the process of manifesting one's reality, even if I still could not completely understand or explain it.

Suddenly, another Realtor sitting in the office asked me what I was looking for. When I told her, she turned to our Realtor and said, "Why don't you call Darlene? Maybe she is ready to sell another villa." It turned out that Darlene owned six villas and sold one a year after her husband's untimely death.

"Great idea!" our Realtor replied, already picking up the

phone. After a brief conversation with Darlene, he said, "Incredible! She was going to call me this week about a villa she's about to put on the market."

This was heartening news, but my needs, I reminded him, were specific. I wanted a particular model with a larger under air-conditioned space but a less covered lanai. It couldn't have a pool and it must be on the water so Chip could enjoy the fish and birds.

"I have the perfect place for you," the Realtor said. "It is the model you wanted, and the tenants are going to leave to go back to Boston to live near their family."

Boston…my twin brother's stomping grounds, I thought, the now familiar chills running down my spine and the hair on my arms standing on end.

As soon as I walked into that villa I knew it was ours. Chip hurried down to the water, calling out like a youngster when he saw the abundance of wildlife. There were butterflies flitting about, fish swimming, ducks gliding and two large magnolia trees were ready to come into full bloom. I think God sent every creature to greet and welcome this prize-winning nature photographer!

The villa also had everything I described on my wish list, including no pool and a double-sized screened in lanai. Added to this was the street number—5579—which, "coincidentally" was very similar to our friends villa on the south side of the community, 5779. Right then, one of my mother and father's favorite songs popped into my mind.

Ah! Sweet Mystery of Life

At Last I've found thee!
Ah! At last I know the secret of it all.
All the longing, seeking, striving, waiting, yearning
The burning hopes, the joy, and idle tears that fall
For 'tis love, and love alone, the world is seeking
And 'tis love, and love alone, that can repay
'Tis the answer, 'tis the end and all of living
For it is love alone that rules for aye.

Was this song providing me with one of the answers I was seeking? Was it all about Love after all—Love of God? Love of the Angels? Love of Spirit? Love of the Universe? And, as Mother Mary had asked me, did I love enough? I did not know, but as I pondered those lyrics I couldn't help but think they were yet another sign.

This, however, is not the end of the story, for this "perfect" villa was in fact not on the market. Yet I made an offer just a bit lower than the asking price and it was accepted within the hour. It would be the wisest decision I'd ever made.

How could I ever doubt that the perfect villa would manifest? Wasn't Spirit/God proving to me that this manifesting works unfailingly?

With the move-in date set for April 1, Chip and I visited our son and his family at his gulf-front summer home on Florida's Panhandle. What a glorious view; the sunsets on the Gulf of Mexico were superb as was the white sand. They had also prepared a Mexican themed party with all Chip's favorite foods. How he loved his tacos, his quesadillas, his beans and rice and all the trimmings! We had a fabulous time, though our adult children and grandchildren had no idea that this was really a farewell birthday party. Chip's condition had begun to accelerate at an alarming pace

"Don't upset the kids," he had told me haltingly and with great effort, "It is going to be a little while." That was his mandate to me when we both realized that this was going to be the end of his life here on earth.

Chip's children would also plan an outstanding eightieth birthday party for him at his daughter's exquisite home in the Atlanta suburbs. It was held in true Georgian style, with home-cooked barbeque and all of his favorite dishes. Chip talked about the food—and the Atlanta Braves baseball game planned by his son—all the way home. What a long, long trip that was, especially since I, now also nearing my eightieth birthday, had to do all the driving.

Once we got back home, the reality of the situation hit me hard. Chip was declining by the day. It was time to put to the test my belief that we are all spiritual beings having a physical experience. I knew our earthbound journey was relatively short, and that we would one day be reunited on the other side. This, however, didn't make it any easier to say goodbye.

How could I ever get through it? Only with the presence of my angels and the Blessed Mother Mary, to whom I prayed consistently. My belief in Jesus and God were unshakable; the Faith that my mother showed upon my father's drawn-out death had set the example.

"Mother Mary," I said aloud, "you saw your son die a horrible death on the cross, so I can get through this. For compared to what you witnessed and suffered, this is nothing!" This would keep my perspective. I also continually prayed that Chip did not suffer any physical pain.

Despite his condition Chip was well aware of what was going on. Once in a while he would talk long into the night, and though the nouns had to be filled in he expressed concern about our pledge to never put one another in an institution. Of course, I would faithfully keep my pledge. I did not make many promises, but those I did make I honored. Chip knew this better than anyone.

One day he became very lucid and talked about what he wanted for a memorial service, emphasizing his wish to be cremated, a Celebration not a funeral and he gave me instructions for his ashes.

He also said he wanted my chorus to sing at the Celebration of his Life. Chip had always loved music, and he loved it when I sang; over our forty years together he had attended most of my rehearsals, whether it was a church choir or a chorus like the Sweet Adelines who sang women's barbershop. As I listened to his requests, including a male Barbershop Quartet which he loved, my heart was breaking. I wasn't at all sure that I could do it.

Finally I had to admit that I needed help in caring for him. I had injured my back from lifting Chip and could no longer shower him. I hired two professional male medical assistants, one for the mornings and one for the evenings.

Behind closed doors it was very apparent how debilitated

Chip had become, yet somehow, he was able to cover it up in front of others. Amazed at first, I eventually reached the conclusion that most people would ask him a question and, in the hesitation that followed, they would just keep talking about themselves, unaware of his struggle to answer. This was especially true during his phone conversation with our children; to them, he had simply become the best listener in the world.

To this point, Chip was always aware of what was happening, but now there was a major shift. His actions were often combative and soon became that of a toddler and I was on a twenty-four-hour-a-day watch. In rare moments of quiet, I began to journal and write a few poems to release some of my pent-up emotions, but oftentimes I was too exhausted to do even that.

I remembered that Hospice had an intermediate program, so I called them in and registered. It was now fall and no volunteers were available. Our children were a Godsend. My son and daughter-in-law lived locally and they would come over on Sundays so I could food shop and run errands. Chip's daughter and son and daughter-in-law came for a week so I could go north and visit my family. They took Chip out for rides, took him to the Gulf, looked at the sunsets and played games with him.

When I returned I called the Veteran's Pinning Team at Hospice and his Marine buddies came to the home and performed his Service that he had done many times for others. There was not a dry eye there. I still see him sitting straight up in his wheelchair and saluting his fellow officers.

As grateful as I was for their help, it was no longer

enough. Feeling alone and overwhelmed, on September 20th, I called Hospice for an evaluation. When they came they were alarmed that I was caring for him by myself, and my explanation that I was a R.N. and had professional help to shower him in the morning and in the evening to go out for walks and get him into bed did nothing to ease their concerns.

"You are fired!" they said kindly, then told me they were bringing in ICU nurses around the clock. These hospice nurses would prove to be angels on earth. I can never praise them enough for their compassionate and competent care of their dear "Captain Chip," who when working at Hospice wore his Navy officer's dress whites to pin dying veterans. Oh, how he loved to attend those ceremonies, which he thought of as God's work.

Now he was being treated with the same reverence having been awarded his pin for his service in the Navy aboard an aircraft carrier. I also was finally getting relief from administering medication, turning and changing him. I was even more grateful for the nurses' honesty.

"You know that he is near the end," the leader told me.

I had known it, but her confirmation lifted a huge burden from my shoulders. I sensed the end was near and I simply could not do it alone anymore. Grief was overtaking me as I looked at his frail, debilitated frame and the sadness on his face.

Now I was free just to sit with him and sing to him and love him. I called a Unity minister that Chip admired, as he had said he wanted to have his service in her church. She came right away and knelt beside his bed, talking and praying with him. While he was never in physical pain, his emotional pain had torn at my heartstrings. Whatever the minister said to him was of the highest order and value, for he was visibly more relaxed and comforted after that.

The end of Chip's life was as filled with love as was the rest of it. The weekend before he died, two of his sons came to visit. That same weekend, our daughter, Amy, also came; she spent time sitting with him and feeding him. This was her "Daddy," the one who had adopted her as his own. I shall never forget how happy it made him to be surrounded by his adult children.

On the second day of Hospice care, he looked up at me and signaled something with his fingers. At first, I was puzzled, then I realized he was forming a cross. When I asked him if he wanted his cross he nodded his head, then said, clear as a bell, "It's time for *this* now."

Gently, I placed the chaplain's cross around his neck. It was the symbol not only of his Christian faith, but of the work he so dearly loved and did in hospitals and hospice.

For the last thirty-plus hours I did not leave his side; I sang his favorite songs, hymns and Christmas Carols and told him funny stories and memories of our travels throughout the states and Europe. I talked about our cruises and especially recounted some really special fun RV and boat trips. Every time I stopped talking or singing he would squeeze my hand tightly…urging me not to stop. I was exhausted.

Can this really be happening? Is this the end of our days together here on earth? There was a part of my mind that thought this was a bad dream and that he would be fine in a short time. This is denial. I did not want him to see me cry so

I left for my 15 minute crying breaks between the songs and stories.

The night nurse, who was beginning her shift just as I started to sing "Silent Night," joined in with the harmony. It was just a beautiful, sacred moment. And it was during that lovely Christmas carol that he looked at me and touched his lips with his fingers. He then placed his fingers on my lips and with a smile went home to be with God.

I stayed with him until about four hours later, though I knew his soul had departed. I could not leave his side until the coroner arrived and draped his body with the American Flag and removed him from our home. The one thing I would not let him do was to cover Chip's face up before he left. It was an odd reaction but he did not like his face covered while alive and I was insistent this was not done. Sadly, I watched as the gurney took away the body of my beloved husband. It was the emptiest feeling in the world...I hurt so much I could barely walk, however the hospice nurse who had stayed gently guided me to our bedroom and said "Go to sleep now...he is in God's hands."

Just before I fell into a deep sleep I realized it was the 26th of September. Chip had waited for my mother's birthday—and the same day my sister's husband had died—to make his transition. I was not sure of the significance of that, though I'd seen enough to know it was certainly no coincidence.

Goodnight, my Dear Prince of a Man. Thank you for forty glorious years, and until we meet again know that I will *always* love you.

Missing In Action

Where are you my love
your eyes are blank
no sign of recognition of me
no glimpse of your sweet soul
You have left yet someone
who looks like you is here.
He is often cruel;
he cannot speak nor understand
a spoon is a banana
Where have you gone?
Pray God will take you home
released from this nightmare
know you have the power
to cross over at will
Do not wait
You are free as the birds
FLY DARLING...FLY!

Elizabeth

For Bobbi, from Chip
(His first attempt at writing poetry 1976)

The world doth gaze upon you
A thousand sides they see
But there's one side of Elizabeth
That's only seen by me.
The moments we spend alone
Are to me sheer ecstasy
Would I have the power
They would last eternally
In my dreams we drift forever
In an endless sea of love
Transcending all around us
The earth below, the sky above.
The memories of the times
When together we did meet
Raises my soul's awareness
And makes my life complete.
How many people trundle
Along their dreary way
And never know the joy
Your love brings me today
The world's at peace around me
There is happiness everywhere
As we embark together
On our life-time love affair.

Elizabeth was Chip's affectionate nickname for me.

With my apologies to Elizabeth Barrett Browning.

A Final Goodbye

You are my true love-the skies of blue
The twinkling stars, the very hue
of flowers' colors gazing at me
The Sunsets and Moonlight that I see
are paler than your shining soul
Soon to traverse to the ultimate goal.
Transitioning
To the Heavenly Plane
Know that your life was not in vain.
For you have given so much to others
Treating all like Sisters and Brothers
The light glimmers from your eyes so blue
Still clearly says to me
"I love you"
The love from your heart still so strong
One for which I still lovingly long
As the parting hour draws nigh, I tear
Because we do not have another year
You will forever be my fall,
my summer, my winter, my spring-
MY ALL.

On Being Alone

I lie here alone in the half-empty bed
Dreams of our life dancing in my head
Thinking of the eternal Love felt for you
Knowing how deeply you Loved me too
It is now that I know that when alone
Your Spirit, your Light and Love are shown
Your gentle and kind ways live in me
And never alone again will I ever be
Though I cannot touch nor see you now
You are here always-I don't know how
Your Thoughts and Being have invaded my soul
And loving and living in the Now is my goal
No matter what keeps us physically apart
You will forever live in the depths of my heart.

Chapter Fourteen

MANIFESTING AFTER DEATH CONTACTS

*C*hip and I had often talked about whether it would be possible to communicate with each other after one left this earthly plane for "the other side." We both promised that whoever died first would try to send signs. Chip said he would try to blink the lights and send butterflies, his favorite nature subject, to me and family members.

After Chip's transition I saw many of these signs, and others in the family reported the presence of butterflies sitting on their shoulders or at their feet for long periods of time. I also noticed that bird feathers started falling at my feet on a regular basis, and though we have never discussed this it was clear that this was also a sign from my husband. Chip loved birds of all kinds and had taken many winning photographs of them.

He also blinked the lights and, ever the skeptic, I would always check the bulb and the electrical connection. In only one case was it a burned-out bulb.

Chip also reached me through music, usually through our favorite *Easy Listening* TV program.

One day when I turned it on and was amazed to hear *The Twelfth of Never*—our song—was just beginning to play. However, I guess because I was taking these contacts very much in stride he decided to amp it up a bit; "our song" was followed by El Condor Pasa ... *I'd Rather Be a Hammer Than A Nail!* This song was one that I heard in the OR, both after my Near Death Experience and during the brain surgery. Now he had my attention!

There were two other events, however, that truly blew my mind and inspired me to research After Death Contacts (ADC) further. I had gone to visit our best friends, who had been away when Chip passed and unable to make the memorial service. One day we were leaving to go out to lunch when all of a sudden, we heard a loud distinctive rushing noise in the sky overhead.

We turned to see three bald eagles flying very low in perfect formation; they were flying so fast that the noise attracted our attention. Surely this must be some kind of message to the three of us from Chip!

Then, while at lunch my friend told me that she had recently found her diamond engagement and wedding rings, which had been missing for over a year. Something, she said, had made her husband search a closet in the laundry room. He had checked this closet before, without success. The shelves were very deep. He emptied each shelf and on the bottom shelf way back in the corner of the right side was a very small open corner. He spotted something...just a glint...that he didn't remember seeing before. Could it be...?

He crouched very low on the floor until he was almost lying on his belly, reached in, and there they were—the diamond engagement ring and the wedding ring!

As my friend told me the story, I couldn't help but

wonder—had Chip somehow produced these? My curiosity piqued, I did a search on Amazon for books on after-death contacts. The sheer number of these books on the subject was incredible. Two in particular—*The FUN of Dying* and *The FUN of Staying in Touch* by Roberta Grimes—caught my eye. How, I wondered, could this be fun?

I immediately ordered the books and anxiously awaited their arrival. When they did, I was not disappointed, as they confirmed all the events that happened to me, and there were many. I present the following story as an example of the possibility of After Death Contacts (ADC).

Chip had now been gone for weeks and I felt the urge to play the organ. During the move to the villa, two wooden pieces of the organ that held my music were loose and unattached. I could not discern where the pieces fit into the organ, and neither could my handyman, so I called the store where I bought the organ. They told me to bring the pieces over and they would show me how to insert them.

When I entered the store with the organ pieces in hand, I was greeted by a pleasant, middle-aged woman who introduced herself as Carolyn. Holding out the organ pieces, I quickly explained my dilemma.

At once, a tall man entered the room and said, "Hi! My name is John ... are you not Chip's wife?"

I told him I was, then informed him of Chip's death.

He offered his condolences, then asked about our family, particularly our grandchildren, some of whom were now college age. I told him of our grandson, also named John, who had recently scored a perfect 800 on the math portion of the SATs.

Both the man and Carolyn were quite in awe of that. "My nephew did that also!" Carolyn said, "Do you know that only one percent of all who take the test get a perfect score?"

I knew it was a slim number, and I thought about the odds of meeting someone else whose relative had done that. I also told them of the scholarship offers John had received, added that he had chosen to attend GA Tech.

When I said those words, Carolyn gasped audibly and put her hand over her mouth. "Oh my!" she exclaimed, "I woke up today singing the GA Tech fight song!" She then proceeded to sing, "He's a hell of a wreck from GA Tech and a hell of an engineer."

I couldn't believe what I was hearing, especially when she told me she didn't even know anyone from GA or GA Tech!

"I told my husband about it," she said, "I told him I cannot get that song out of my mind! Wait until I tell him what happened!"

I talked to her a little bit about these kinds of occurrences and gave her the name of Edgar Cayce's book, *There is a River,* which in my opinion is a good place to start any metaphysical study. I also told her that I did not understand how these things happen but that I recognize that they do and record the significant ones. This synchronicity around the GA Tech story, I felt, was confirmation that Chip knew of our grandson's choice of schools and was letting us know how proud he was of him.

After all, Georgia Tech was Chip's and his mother's

alma mater!

It was then that John announced he would come to my home and insert the pieces back into the organ. He also informed me that I had free lessons for life, which of course was what Chip had wanted me to do.

Still overcome by our odd exchange, Carolyn walked out of the store with me. We chatted for a short while and I pointed her to some online sites on metaphysics.

In time, I did begin taking organ lessons; I even updated to a larger model once I realized the technology was so advanced. The front of the organ looks like a cockpit of an airplane. I can play the notes easily but am studying diligently how to work all the buttons and whistles!

When I returned for the lessons I learned Carolyn had left the job. A recent transfer from Manhattan and a veteran of the music industry, she was no doubt looking for something more challenging. However, I believe that God placed her there so she could confirm Chip's acknowledgement of our grandson's school choice and I could raise her consciousness and enlighten her as to the possibilities beyond the physical world. We were each other's messengers.

"Coincidence is God's way of remaining anonymous."
~Albert Einstein

Over the next two years I would have several other ADC experiences with my beloved husband, which I recorded in my journal. I include the entries below.

May 14, 2016

UNBELIEVABLE! I had just finished kissing his small pic goodnight ... it is 12:12 a.m. on 5/14/16 ... it has been 8 months since he crossed over ... I know his soul exists...he lives ... he answers me all the time ... tonight I was so frustrated b/c I had looked all day for my glasses ... under the bed with a flashlight ... under the nightstand ... I put them on the nightstand at night or his dresser ... I asked, "Please Chip help me find my glasses," ... he answered, "Look Down!" and there, neatly placed between the frame of the bed and the mattress, were my glasses! Now that was right next to the bedside stand that I was searching under and that side of the bed, with a flashlight ... they were not there ... not only that they were neatly folded ... and the glasses were facing out ... like a magician had produced them ... in the flicker of an eye ... and Chip was an amateur magician ... I really thought I heard him chuckle.

I cried when I found them and then laughed ... OMG! I miss him so but he continues to amaze me. I love him so and know he is showing off his abilities to connect with me ... like right now when the computer is moving the line backwards as I type ... it is incredible! I am going to look up in the book whether people can influence computers! LOL! It says it can happen! Why am I crying? Because I miss our deep conversations ... oh, I see that he jumped it to the center setting ... that is what has happened ... and he changes the font ... thinks it is fun! Could that really be possible?

June 2016

I had not heard from Chip for a while but now suddenly feathers were being dropped again. As I walked the beach we so often visited feathers were presented at my feet seemingly out of nowhere. I am seeing that as a sign that he likes the fact I am getting out to the beach and walking as I was severely injured (fractured tibia and torn tissue of 6 vertebrae) and had not been able to do it for quite a while.

November 11, 2017

I woke up early with the clear message:

"Make the book cover the color of my favorite book, The One by Richard Bach, name it Manifesting Miracles, and use the dove I gave to you in exchange for my chaplain's cross on the cover."

There was no doubt Chip was communicating with me. The dove had been very significant in his life. He had even gone to a jeweler and sketched to size the dove that he wanted made up in gold. It would be surrounded by a circle of gold and he wore it on a gold chain every day of his life.

After receiving the message I was immediately compelled to sit and crudely sketch a dove with ribbons floating from it and a circle around it. I don't know why I drew that image with ribbons. I placed small sparkles of silver all around the image. That, my friends, is what you see represented on the cover of this book. To me, it is a prayer for peace in our world.

I did not know what to do with the logo I sketched, but

he answered my question: *Send it to a company on the net.* He then named the company. As his messages are always clear, I got on the web and found that I could send my ideas to a graphic artist and some samples would be returned for my review. That is how I developed my present logo, which I dearly love.

NOTE:

As mentioned earlier, when Chip lay in his hospice bed that dove was exchanged for his chaplain's cross. That same day he also indicated by hand motions that he wanted me to wear the dove. I put the dove on my gold omega and placed it around my neck. I view it as a sign of the peace I dearly pray will come in my lifetime.

April 24, 2018

I have not heard from Chip in a long while; I have the sense he is very busy...probably working on world peace. Today is his birthday. OMG! I walked out to my car and there is a small gray feather on the hood! How could it get in my garage that has not been opened since last night...it is to me a precious sign that he knows all about my life and is so happy that I am managing to have fun and have adjusted to my new status. It is still on my dresser to remind me to keep writing! The others he sent are stored in lovely Shaker boxes my twin brother made.

When I have the time, I am going to re-read the books on After Death Contacts as I just perused them for confirmation. Perhaps I will be able to gather more information as it is a field that holds my interest. Perhaps we can share stories in the future.

June 20, 2018

I have not heard from Chip in a while. Suddenly two things happened in one week. A medium sized white bird feather appeared on my floor near the breakfast bar where I could not miss it! There were no birds in my home (LOL!) and it was not there the night before as I carefully check the house each night before going to bed.

The second occurrence was this: My grandson and I were being playful; he said he loved me and I responded, "I love you to the moon and back" and he said, "I love you more" and I said, "I love you to infinity!" and he responded, "I can't beat that!"

The next morning on my massage table, square in the middle, was a small silver round piece of jewelry a bit larger than the size of a dime. On it was written, "I love you to the moon and back!" It was not there the night before. How, who, what or where did it come from?

Chapter Fifteen

MANIFESTING A NEW RELATIONSHIP

*D*ecades ago, a widowed friend had remarked to me, "The world is built for twosies." Now that Chip was gone, I was experiencing the truth of her observation firsthand. Time, which had passed all too quickly when we were together, now seemed to drag. Bridge, exercise, book clubs, music and other art pursuits.

I kept very busy, with bridge and exercise groups, book clubs and music and other artistic pursuits. But later in the evening, when the sun was sinking in the west, after all was quiet, I began to feel lonely. Tired of the talking heads on TV, I would watch many of our old favorite movies. What I really longed for, though, was someone to talk to; someone to confide in, or to even care whether I had arrived home safely.

Most of my friendships centered on the activity we were engaged in and went no further. I had some dear girlfriends, most of whom were married. So many of my dearest friends had gone to live with their families or had gone home to be with God.

My friends who were not married were fifteen years younger and comfortable in the club scene and singles nights. There were also plenty of singles groups in the town. I went to one travel group and there were over one hundred women and about four old men. I almost ran out but I had to take a friend home and she was busy signing up for a trip to France.

I had always enjoyed male conversation and company. I found men more interested in world affairs and the political climate of our nation. I also liked to talk to them about their careers. I know that sounds sexist but my generation of women are different than my daughters' generation. I still enjoy men and really wanted to travel again but not with a gaggle of gabbing girls!

You have to understand that it was not codependency; I always felt that I was equal to a man, perhaps because I had a twin brother. I simply was not happy about giving up the pedestal most men my age put women on.

I first tried the online dating sites—*that* experience alone could fill another book. I listed the qualities of the man whom I wanted to meet: honesty and integrity, a good communicator with a sense of humor, someone who was conservative in philosophy, a non-smoker, spiritual, who liked to travel and enjoyed music and theatre.

Basically, I wanted to meet someone that most women wanted to meet. What set my requirements apart was the age group of seventy-five to eighty-nine, within ten miles from my home. I also required at least a college degree and preferably a post- graduate degree.

Some of the communications were so outrageous I laugh-ed all morning after reading them. Others were pretty wild and fairly amorous, considering I was an unknown entity. It simply was not believable. Although I did meet one or two very interesting men it was hard to meet someone who was initially interested in friendship with the possibility of a long-term relationship in the future. I was not interested in marriage, but in companionship. I did meet one man I liked very much and dated for a short while, but we were definitely not a philosophical match. I decided to "put it out there," then let it go and concentrate on my present life, just as I had done so many times before.

And that's exactly what I did. I threw myself into the chorus, which was back in rehearsal for the Christmas show; I was writing poetry again and decided to start a published poet's group. I also decided to write another book and bought that new organ to take advanced lessons. I even joined a Bunco group, where I met eleven new women of diverse professions and a whole lot of fun. When I felt like travelling, I had friends and family all over the country to visit.

It hadn't been easy, but I had created a new life without my beloved Chip, and it was a happy one. After a while, I decided I didn't even have time for a man.

I forgot that as soon as you let go and let God, things begin to happen. This time God, Spirit and the Angels would outdo themselves!

One day about a month after I had written down my manifestation I stopped to get my nails done. It was a salon I had seldom visited since I moved, and as I eased myself into the pedicure chair, in walked an attractive young woman who looked a bit familiar to me. We began chatting, and I learned her name was Alexandra and that she lived in the community that had bordered my backyard for decades. We believed we had crossed paths but did not know where.

The conversation then turned to Alexandra's son, who

was visually impaired. I mentioned that my niece Nancy had taught students at The Perkins School in Massachusetts. Founded in 1829, the school counted Helen Keller among its students and to this day remained one of the best institutions of its kind in the United States. It was also more than a thousand miles away, so I was a bit surprised when Alexandra told me she had visited. The synchronicity had begun!

Though in the end they had chosen a program closer to home, I offered to have my niece check out her son's ophthalmologist, as she knew them all.

We had an instant rapport, this young woman and I, moving easily from subject to subject. We even talked about the real estate business, as Alexandra was studying for her Real Estate Broker's examination, which I had taken myself years earlier.

I was so enjoying our conversation when suddenly she said, "You have to meet a close friend of my late mother's. You just have to! He is so nice, so much fun and I do not want him to be alone. My mother died over two years ago. Do you think you would like to meet him?"

She threw the questions at me in rapid succession, catching me completely off-guard. I told her I was too busy to get involved with anyone, and in fact I had recently decided I did not want a man in my life. But she wouldn't take no for an answer.

"Oh, I know you would really like him!" Alexandra said with enthusiasm. "He is a father figure to me...I love him!"

Hmmm... If she thought he was that nice perhaps it wouldn't hurt to meet him. Instead, though, I found myself asking, "Is he financially stable?" Normally this wouldn't be a thought, but I had met a few men online who were definitely looking for a nurse and a purse. I had also been forewarned of that by my girlfriends, hence my caution.

"Oh, yes," she replied emphatically, "He owns a home here and is retired from an excellent corporate job!"

"Is he fat?" I asked, now feeling a bit ridiculous.

Alexandra just laughed. "No, he is fit…plays tennis three times a week." She paused. "You know, I think he would like you and you him…you remind me of my mother."

Wow! That was quite a statement, one I did not know whether I could live up to, or even wanted to, for that matter.

Alexandra was looking at me expectantly. "Well?"

She really was a lovely young woman, and I couldn't help but think that this man she so deeply cared about had to be a quality person as well.

"Oh, okay," I said finally as I pulled a business card from my person and handed it to her. "Have him call me if he is interested."

I left the salon happy to have met Alexandra, though I didn't dwell much on her matchmaking efforts. In fact, I promptly forgot about it as I focused on my growing list of activities. Topping that list was this book – I had started the outline, was planning to take another writing course, and was signed up for an online publishing seminar.

Spirit, however, did not care about my to-do list; Spirit was working on that which I had already put out there to manifest.

Within a week of that fateful pedicure, my phone rang.

"Bobbi?" said a deep male voice, "This is Paul, Alexandra's friend. She said she thought you and I should meet."

My stomach was doing flip-flops and my mind was racing. *Oh, no! What the heck did I get myself into? I Should have said no! I am so busy with deadlines.*

I took a deep breath and gathered my wits about me. "Oh, yes. She thought we should meet and I would enjoy that." As I said the words, I realized it was the truth. He had a beautiful speaking voice and I had to admit I was quite intrigued.

Once I agreed to the meeting, Paul took charge of the conversation. He already had the restaurant picked out and even suggested a day. It was a trait I had always liked in a man. It also happened that on the day he chose I would be about five doors away at my beauty parlor. *Oh...oh...here we go! I do believe the Universe is manifesting!*

That day, when I walked the short distance to our meeting place, I glanced at an attractive man with beautiful silver white hair and I kept on walking. He had said he was grey haired. Suddenly, I got the feeling it may be him and slowed my step.

"Paul?"

The man looked at me. "Bobbi?"

What was to be our short meet and greet turned out to be a two-and-a-half-hour marathon lunch. My immediate impression was that he was a very nice guy. Paul was also handsome in a manly way—not a pretty boy—and even had beautiful hands. He surely had the gift of gab as well, and our conversation flowed easily. He was of Irish descent and originally from the Boston area, where my twin brother and his family now lived. He had that accent I so enjoyed, and then there was that deep voice that had captured my attention when we first spoke me on the phone. Most importantly, I had the sense that he was not a "player," nor one who played head games, both of which would have been a deal-breaker.

We sat there, eating and talking until the staff told us they were closing the restaurant. Then we asked if we could move to their deck while they went about their cleaning duties. As we sat there, overlooking the water, I realized I was having a wonderful time. When he asked if he could see me again, I did not even hesitate before saying yes.

Of course, this story would not be complete without the many incredible synchronicities that revealed themselves as we spoke.

To start with, Paul's daughter had graduated from the same small school of nursing in New Jersey I had attended decades earlier. He had also earned his M.B.A. from the same university where I received my baccalaureate degree! And there was still more—four of my children had been born in the same town where he had lived with his late wife, who was also—you guessed it, a nurse!

Another of his daughters and her husband lived with their three daughters in the small rural town in New Jersey where my brother and his wife, also a graduate of our school of nursing, had brought up their three daughters.

There were also more synchronicities concerning Alexandra—I would later discover that she too had graduated from my alma mater, and my daughter rode horses and competed in horse shows at the same stable as she did, though she lived about twenty miles away!

Paul and I had other things in common as well. We both loved certain sports cars but followed out practical natures and drove Hondas. And from that first conversation, it was apparent that we thought a lot alike and often said the same thing at the same time. When Paul told me the name of his community and street name, I nearly gasped aloud. Not only did we live in the same town, but the name of his street and community was the same as the Director of my school of nursing!

Okay, God, now you are blowing my mind!

And so it went, with so many synchronicities they are too numerous to name. Paul also lived up to that first impression, and at the time of this writing we have been dating for over a year and in July while vacationing in the mountains of NC we made it formal when he gifted me with a ring. We now reside together.

Paul is a gentleman and a scholar. He is very kind, thoughtful, gallant, romantic, and has a wicked sense of humor. He and I like the same movies, enjoy theatre and music; we like to cook at home, and go to good ethnic restaurants.

I especially enjoy his command of history. It was a topic I had always been interested in; unfortunately, in high school I had a lackluster American History teacher whose primary intent was to have us memorize the dates of Civil War battles.

I did, however, have a fabulous teacher who taught a

contemporary history course called Problems of American Democracy, a fascinating exploration of World War II and the Cold War eras. I was exposed weekly to President Roosevelt's fireside chats and Walter Winchell, who began his show with, "Good evening. Mr. and Mrs. North and South America and all the ships at sea. Let's go to press."

I also read the newspaper every day, and wrote at least three times a week to my favorite cousin, who was serving in the War. Those were both scary and fascinating times.

Now that I am older I have grown to appreciate the history of our country's founding, and have found Paul to be a treasure trove. He's a student of the history of almost everything, but he's especially fond of American History. When we're together he enjoys giving me mini-history lessons almost as much as I enjoy listening to them.

Paul also shares my love of travelling, and my love of trains as well.

It has not escaped my notice that Chip had many of the same traits. Part of this is due to the fact that they are of the same generation; however, they are also that rare breed of men—strong of character and heart—that dreams are made of. Indeed, Chip would have liked Paul very much, and Paul, who also lost someone dear, understands how much I miss him. We talk often and easily of our spouses, which is very comforting.

We also talk freely about the different kinds of love we have experienced throughout our lives. Now in our sunset years, we live full of gratitude that we enjoy good health and that we found someone wonderful to love. That said, we also agree that marriage at our ages would not be of benefit to either one of us and only complicate our lives. Instead, we are just content taking one day at a time and enjoying each and every moment we have together. It is my hopes that we have many wonderful years ahead of us.

A Divine Match

A Heart
Locked for years
Fears
and
Salty tears
Could not bear pain
Nor hurt again
Then you
entered my life
No sorrow
No strife
Secrets shared
Souls bared
Meeting like this
Divine Bliss!

The Awakening Soul

Arriving with a poinsettia at his side
My heart gave a lurch; it opened so wide
Unexpectedly, my feelings stirred once more
They were sleeping—unnoticed in my very core
Delicate red petals so lovely were they
Reflecting the beauty of the Holy Day.
Hard to remember when flowers were received.
Except by those who joined me when grieved.
Feeling an exquisite joy I cannot explain
For buried deep my emotions had been lain.
Something stirred strongly in my soul tonight
Filled with the gifts of Love and Light.

Chapter Sixteen

MANIFESTING MY SOUL'S DESIRE

*T*hough I was born a Baptist and later became a Methodist; I attended church regularly as a child and teenager, and this continued into adulthood. I would also bring my own children up in the Methodist church. Yet, in one way or another, Catholicism had always been a part of my life.

My best childhood friend Mary, who lived just up the street from me, was a Catholic. We studied the questions of the Catechism together and I often accompanied her to confession on Friday afternoons. While she was waiting for the priest I would sit in the pew and gaze at the beauty of the stained-glass windows. Tentatively, I often pulled down the kneeling bench to say a prayer.

As a teenager I dated Roman Catholic boys and attended their high school proms. During my three years of nursing education, I was the only Protestant member of the Newman Club, which is a Catholic student organization on college campuses. Their purpose is to encourage each other and teach what it means to be a Catholic.

It was there I was exposed to the Saints. My favorite prayer is that of St. Francis of Assisi. That is the name the current Pope took. To me he personifies the humility of St. Francis.

The Peace Prayer of Saint Francis
(1182–1226)

Lord, make me an instrument of your peace.
Where there is hatred, let me sow love;
Where there is error, truth;
Where there is injury, pardon;
Where there is doubt, faith;
Where there is despair, hope;
Where there is darkness, light;
And where there is sadness, joy.
O Divine Master, grant that I may not so much seek
To be consoled as to console;
To be understood as to understand;
To be loved as to love.
For it is in giving that we receive;
It is in pardoning that we are pardoned;
It is in self-forgetting that we find;
And it is in dying to ourselves that we are born
to eternal life.
Amen.

The author of this classic prayer is unknown, yet, in 1920 it was ascribed to Saint Francis when found on the back of one of his cards.

It was during my marriage to Chip that we discovered *The Hour of Power* with Dr. Robert Schuller and the Crystal Cathedral. Frankly, we worked very hard during the week and had no desire to attend church.

His focus was the power of positive thinking and it was just perfect for us at the time.

As I mentioned earlier, after retiring to Florida, Chip and I attended an Episcopal church for a few years, but when our favorite priest left we found something was missing.

We then began church–shopping, mostly amongst Protestant churches, including A Center for Positive Living and The Church of Religious Science. We eventually chose to become members of a Unity Church. Their philosophy is described in Wikipedia as a "positive, practical Christianity" that "teaches the effective daily application of the principles of Truth taught and exemplified by Jesus Christ" and promotes "a way of life that leads to health, prosperity, happiness, and peace of mind." It was a good choice for us at the time. I filled my soul by singing in the choir, as mentioned, and serving as a chaplain for one year.

During a memorial service for one of our very young chaplains, Kathy, who had died from cancer, I distinctly heard my inner voice urging me to "step forward." Yet it would take almost another year of prayer and contemplation to do so, and then it was arranged by God.

One Sunday morning, we packed our car full of stuff for the annual church garage sale. As we were about to leave for church, Chip suddenly felt nauseated and was not up to going. I would have to go alone and rely on the men of the church to empty my car and trunk. Looking back now, I know how serendipitous these events were.

I sat down in the church pew, alone for the first time, and reviewed the bulletin. There it was, light dancing on it, the announcement said that today was the last Sunday for interviews for the Chaplaincy Program. I looked over the dates for the sixty-hour course plus two retreats. Nothing on my calendar interfered. It was then I got goosebumps up my spine. This was God's way of getting me to do the work I was sent here to do. And so I went for the interview that day and was accepted into the program. My journey as a chaplain had begun.

After our sixty-hour training and retreat we were inducted one Sunday morning during the church service. We stood with candles held in our hands while these words were spoken.

"Then I heard the voice of the Lord saying,

Whom shall I send, and who will go for us?"

Isaiah 6:8

We four soon-to-be-inducted chaplains then sang a refrain of a beautiful hymn by Lannie Burt and Diane Williams:

"Here I am, Lord. It is I Lord?
I have heard you calling in the night.
I will go, Lord, if you lead me.
I will hold your people in my heart"

The minister then placed our white satin stoles around our shoulders and said the closing blessing.

Where would I be led? I did not know. It had taken me almost three years to answer the call to become a chaplain. It was a wonderful year. The people would come after the church service to pray with the chaplain on call.

Yet, I still felt constrained; I was not talking about Jesus the way I knew Him, nor was I praying the way I knew best—from the heart. Our prayers followed a set format and for me the feelings from my soul were not being spoken. Absent for me was the talking about the promise of Jesus and the meaning of the crucifixion.

I was also missing the feeling of entering a sacred and serene space within the building. It was warm and hospitable but absent were the signs of Christianity—the beautiful artifacts and altar I longed to see. I was looking for my stained-glass windows! The people in the church were lovely, the service was enjoyable and it brought me closer to God. However, my soul was not being fed. My major objections were that I differed with the philosophy and view of Jesus, the absence of the Trinity and the belief in transubstantiation during the Communion ritual.

I was also *missing* the ritual of Communion, the Palm Sunday and the Christian Easter Celebrations with *"Christ the Lord is Risen Today"* ringing in my ears! Our Christmas Eve and Christmas Day services were very different in tone, and it was clear I was a misfit for this brand of Christianity! However, my husband was enjoying his role in the church and his writing of the few periodicals and occasional sermon he was called upon to do kept him busy.

During this period, Chip and I traveled very extensively both in the United States and abroad. We went on two dozen cruises to everywhere we could squeeze in. Before one of the cruises we flew to Rome for a week—which for me was an incredible experience and the highlight of my travels. While visiting the Vatican we lit nine very thick, tall, perpetual candles for our children. We listened to masses said in other languages and finally one of my lifetime wishes—to visit the Sistine Chapel—was granted.

I felt like I was standing in a history book. At this time the magnificent ceiling was being restored and the new colors of red, yellow, blue, black and brown looked so bright compared to the centuries-old faded painted scenes and figures. Nevertheless, I had tears in my eyes as I viewed the incredible amount of paintings that one man did while lying on his back on scaffolds. As I stood there, taking it all in, I was overcome with gratitude. It was all I thought it would be.

Our travels also took us to Ephesus, Turkey. It is the most exquisite city I have ever seen. The whole city's edifices and roads are made of white marble, and I could envision the horse- drawn chariots of the day traversing them. Ephesus is also the city where St. Paul began his preaching and there is a mini colosseum there. These trips filled my heart and soul with a sense of wonder and increased my desire to attend an old-fashioned Christian church again.

We also climbed up the hill overlooking the city to see the little wooden shack where it is said St. John hid the Blessed Mother Mary after the crucifixion. It is two barren rooms with nothing but tall candles burning on a table in the exit hallway. I said out loud to my husband, "I wonder if that is true that John brought Mother Mary here?" I am ever the skeptic!

With that question, that others heard, all of the lit candle flames began to flicker—it was if they were dancing. One woman quipped, "Well, I guess you got your answer!" and we all chuckled.

On another trip we went to Portugal and visited Fatima, a town north of Lisbon, where one of the most important Catholic shrines in the world is dedicated to the Virgin Mary. The church was built in memory of the three shepherd children who had claimed to have seen visions of Mother Mary on May 13, 1917 and then again for five more months, always appearing on the 13th day of the month. They were declared "worthy of belief" in 1930. Catholics in America maintain a strong devotion to Mother Mary under the title of Our Lady of Fatima.

In 1981, *on the very same day as the first apparition* of our Lady of Fatima, there was a near fatal assassination attempt on St. John Paul II, the Pope. He was known for his deep and abiding love for the Blessed Mother Mary and credited her with his survival, saying, "It was a mother's hand that guided the bullet's path."

After those trips to Rome, Portugal and Turkey, I wanted to become a Catholic but something always stopped me. In my mind I believed it was my mother who was a strong Baptist and Methodist but I now know that it was me. She would understand now as today she has many Catholic grandchildren and great grandchildren.

After those trips to Europe, we remained in the Unity Church. My husband was happy there and could contribute his energy, his time, his prayers, his speaking, his writing and financial help to enlarge the building. We stayed until my husband's role there as an ordained minister and Hospital Chaplain were apparently not needed any longer as new and younger people would come in to help. He would devote the remainder of his life to serving Hospice.

During my husband's illness, we led a Christian life at home. After his death I floundered for a short while, but everything changed when on Easter Sunday of 2016 I entered the local Roman Catholic Church. I felt, quite simply, that I had come home. It was there I could communicate with the Blessed Mother Mary who was revered and honored by me, and the various Saints and Archangels that were part of my life. It was there I felt the closest to Jesus and God.

I had now flirted with converting to Catholicism for almost two decades and recently a friend brought me a rosary that was blessed by Pope Francis. I treasure that rosary, as well as one crocheted in shades of pink by a friend who gave it to me when I was ill in my thirties. Phyllis may be in heaven but her gift of the hand-crafted rosary is one of my most precious possessions.

Finally, after attending the Roman Catholic Church and comparing it to some others of Protestant faith I felt that I was definitely going to convert to Catholicism and I did not care what anyone said or thought...I was going to satisfy my own heart and soul.

Below are my notes on my Conversion:

December 10, 2017

The time had arrived. I have an appointment with Father J., the senior priest in the morning at 10:00 a.m. to talk about Converting to Catholicism; something I have flirted with and thought about for about twenty years. Always there was someone else's opinion, mostly from my childhood, holding me back. Now I felt free to make up my own mind.

Since Easter of 2016 I have been reading and praying about this decision. Last night I prayed very long and hard for discernment, for wisdom and for guidance. I prayed for God to send me a sign that I was on the right path. This morning I felt God had sent the answer to me. I would attend a Protestant service at 10:00 a.m. and then go to the late mass at 11:30 a.m.

On the way over to the Catholic Church I again prayed for a sign to tell me that I was making the right choice. I pulled into the parking lot and got out of the car. On the sidewalk approaching the front of the car was a young woman, of about fifty years of age, coming into view. I said good morning to her and asked if she was alone. She said yes and asked if I would like to sit with her. She told me it was her first visit to this church.

We chatted easily together while walking to the church. She was from the next town. I told her I was here as a possible convert. She revealed *that she was brought up a Methodist as was I and she had converted to Catholicism in 1994! She also revealed in a later conversation that she was from New Jersey! My home state!* God, how perfect are you? My prayer for a sign was fully and completely answered.

Entering the cathedral, I was again in awe of the beauty expressed in the architecture and the stained-glass windows as well as the art on the walls. There were friendly greeters everywhere! The church was filled with light and the high energy and love was palpable. I was immediately "at home." Why had my search taken so long? We sat together, my new "friend" and I. Interesting that I have never seen her since that morning.

I liked the homily, given by a priest I did not know. He had quite a sense of humor and made the Book of Luke come to life. His message was interwoven with a personal story and it was very good. The choir voices were wonderful and the cantor had an exquisite voice. The thing I loved best was that this was a church where all of the responses were sung, including *The Lord's Prayer*. I just loved it and my eyes were filled with tears as we finished the singing. I clearly loved the symbols and believed that this was the religion that spoke to my soul.

The time had arrived. I was resolute in my decision. I wrote my adult children a letter telling them of my intentions after I made an appointment with the Senior Priest. I will see him in the Morning at 10.00 a.m. to talk about Converting to Catholicism.

The meeting went very well. I was not at all apprehensive and that priest will forever have a fan as he thought my age to be much younger. What a boost for an old woman's ego! Soon the meeting was over and I would be on my way to a one-on-one education in the church's doctrines.

The first meeting is with my teacher, named Mary, of course, who will direct me with my Conversion. The meeting was long and our discussion centered on my spiritual journey.

She is a lovely, gentle, devout woman who has been called to do this work; she loves her role in the church and is clearly gaining much joy as she guides us through this process. Thankfully, she has a delightful sense of humor and that lightens me up as I am fairly anxious about what I have to learn and to do.

It is now Lent. I have another meeting scheduled with Mary and others who are also converting. Though the feeling of homecoming was stronger than ever, at the Sunday Mass after the meeting I asked for a sign from God that I was in the right place.

As I picked up the *Order of Service* and glanced at the bulletin I saw the hymn, *"Here I Am Lord."* Immediately, my body reacted with goosebumps, or "God bumps" as I have started to call them. I almost start to cry as the memory of me singing those words during my induction as a chaplain flashes in my mind. I can still see me with a candle held in one hand and our white satin stoles draped over our shoulders singing:

Here I am, Lord. It is I Lord.
I have heard you calling in the night.
I will go, Lord, if you lead me.
I will hold your people in my heart

Ah! The sweet mystery of Life...the Divine Synchronicity of God...the answers one hears when a consciousness is raised. Now years later, in the middle of my journey to Catholicism, I was singing the same words. How beautiful a tune; how soulful the voices; how full is my heart.

Soon it will be Ash Wednesday...Lent will begin. This may sound silly, but at last I will have ashes put on my forehead in the sign of the cross—a sign of repentance and humility—and yet I am worried about what the appropriate attire is! I think my clothing needs to match this somber occasion. I search the internet to see if I can find something out about the colors to wear. I settle on purple and black.

We are having a soup and bread dinner before the Lenten Service this evening while I meet with others who are converting. Mary, my teacher, will be there. I have a bit of anxiety as to what to do as I am very hungry and getting a bit dizzy in the late afternoon. I have not eaten since dinner last evening except for water. I call my sponsor and I am told that it is okay, because of my age and a medication I take, to eat something. Whew! I quickly grab a hard-boiled egg and some tea. It does make me feel better.

Soon it is 5:00 p.m. and I am on my way to the supper. Much to my surprise people are dressed just as any ordinary day…even a pair of jeans is present. This is great…no worry about appearances. Gone are the old days of covered heads and dresses.

I am relieved as I spot two crockpots full of delicious soups and a basket of freshly made bread with butter. Now I relax and the hunger subsides as I consume two bowls of hearty vegetable soup. The company is lovely and people seem thrilled that we are coming into the RC religion. We are told we inspire what they take for granted being as they call it "Cradle Catholics."

Questions and answers abound, a lot about next Sunday, when we will all go to the large Cathedral after our Mass and be greeted by the Bishop. Ten counties who represent the Diocese will be in attendance with their new prospective members. It will be quite a celebration!

Following the delicious supper, we go to Ash Wednesday

Mass and before I know it, it is my turn to go up and get the sign of the cross made on my forehead. The ashes, I am aware of from my self-study, are made from last year's palms that were blessed in the church on Palm Sunday. According to Christian tradition palm branches were waved at the triumphal entry of Jesus into Jerusalem.

When the ashes are placed on my forehead my eyes fill with tears. I did not anticipate that reaction however my soul is touched at this service. As the sign of the cross is made, the priest repeats Genesis 3:19: "For dust you are and to dust you shall return." I think of Chip.

Music has followed me all during this process of conversion.

It was of course, synchronous that Paul happened to be a Roman Catholic since birth. He encouraged me in every way. After talking with him about the synchronicity of the music, we talked about our favorite hymns. It was not unusual to discover that we both loved *Just a Closer Walk with Thee.* Unfortunately, he would be absent from my Confirmation service due to a death of a young family member in Ohio.

Somehow, I thought it was fitting that I was alone. He was no part of my decision to convert to Catholicism; it was a gradual and personal decision between me and God.

Now as I looked down at the bulletin to sing the next hymn we would sing *Just a Closer Walk with Thee.*

I am weak but thou art strong
Jesus, keep me from all wrong
I'll be satisfied as long

As I walk, let me walk close to Thee.

Just a closer walk with thee
Grant it, Jesus, is my plea
Daily walking close to thee
Let it be, dear Lord, let it be.

And when my feeble life is o'er
And time for me shall be no more
Guide me gently, safely o'er
To thy kingdom's shore, to thy shore.

As we sing, I am completely overwhelmed at this affirmation through music that I am making the right choice. I could not have scripted it better had I chosen the hymn myself! I have been to Mass every Sunday and I especially love the fact that there is so much singing during the service by the parishioners. All responses are sung and hundreds of parishioners singing favorite old hymns move me and make my soul sing.

Soon it is Sunday again, and time to meet the Bishop of the Diocese. It would be a long day, as we were to be introduced to our congregation at 11:30 mass, then proceed to a 2:00 service with the prospective members from over thirty Southwest Florida counties who were also there to meet the Bishop. It was a very touching service as each group walked up with the flag of their church held high before them. It was well organized and soon we would be called up for our turn. The Bishop signaled me to stand next to him and I did for the photo op. It was all good. I was not anxious at all.

When it was time for the closing hymn, I looked down at the bulletin and gasped. We were to sing *On Eagle's Wings,* a hymn sung at Chip's memorial service. An outstanding photo he had captured of an eagle perched on a tree in the Canadian Rockies graced the altar on a stand at his memorial service.

The refrain, now ringing out through the diocese Cathedral, brought tears to my eyes. Gosh, for a non-crier I sure am shedding a lot of tears during this process of conversion.

And He will raise you up on eagles' wings
Bear you on the breath of dawn
Make you to shine like the sun
And hold you in the palm of His hand.

I felt Chip's presence and knew that he was happy for me.

I, along with hundreds of others, would be confirmed at a Palm Sunday Eve Vigil candlelight service. That evening was memorable in every way. We were asked to process down the center aisle with the priests, deacons and altar boys and girls out to a garden that I had never seen. As I went out the French doors I saw a sign that read *"Welcome to Mary's Garden!"* and a chill ran up and down my spine. God bumps appeared on my arms and tears once again filled my eyes.

The view before me took my breath away. The sweet fragrance of flowers filled the air. Hundreds of white lilies, impatiens and other flowers in shades of pink, white and purple had been planted by volunteers that day. They were in full bloom and surrounded an exquisite elevated statue of the Blessed Mother Mary. The flowers flowed around her feet and lined the walkways and walls around the garden. It was a lovely Easter tribute.

As I gazed up during the lighting of the oversized Christian candle, the glow reflected onto Mother Mary's face and also formed a beautiful halo around her head. As her face looked down at me I felt a profound sense of completion. After a short ceremony we processed out holding lighted candles and entered the main church for our Confirmation. The hundreds of congregants all held lit candles in their hands. It was a very special spiritual moment.

The Confirmation would be held on the altar of the church. It was also adorned with dozens of white lilies. It was a beautiful, grace-filled moment. As the sacred oil was placed in the shape of a small cross on my forehead by the priest I was filled with a profound sense of, peace and love.

I believe the Blessed Mother Mary's challenge to me has been fulfilled and my soul's mission is completed.

EPILOGUE

"You have just begun your journey, my dear."

*T*he Blessed Mother Mary was so precise when she said those words to me seventeen years ago. Little did I know the joy and sorrow that I would experience since that day. I certainly had no plans to write another book, write more poetry, be the founder of a published poetry group, nor become a widow. Most importantly, I did not anticipate a reunion with my grandson nor the beautiful great-grandchildren that I would live to see born.

And so, this circle has been completed. I do anticipate much more synchronicity and extraordinary coincidences in my lifetime.

I urge you to be aware of the "coincidences" in your life and realize that they are actually much more than that.

LET'S DISCUSS!

I would like to hear about your stories and perhaps gather them for another book if you give me permission to do so. I will only use your first name if you desire, or another name of your choice.

If you are interested in sharing your stories or wish to

contact me, visit my website at:

www.manifestingmiraclesbook.com

A Very Special Post-Humous Dedication

to

Alexandra, Our Beloved Matchmaker

and

Sherril, Our Dear Friend And Fellow Nurse

May they rest in love and light in the arms
of the angels.

The Fall Brides

Two weddings scheduled for this fall...oh my!
One ocean-front at Cape Cod and another near-by
The two young women - so happy were they
Planning for their soon to be wedding day
Each bride fifty-eight years of age
Now ready to turn another page
Divorced over a decade-professionals known
Each had two children now fully grown
Their beaus - both handsome men are they
Who had looked for their soul mate every day
September and October - just one month apart
Both would give to another their heart
The one who introduced us would fall ill
On her wedding day heaven, she would fill
September now became a month to grieve
Her friends and loved ones she would leave
To join others who had passed before
Up to the heavens her soul would soar
Wondering how we could face the October bride
We once again were among those that cried
For she too fell ill and on her wedding day
She greeted guests - a final farewell to pay
Bidding a sad goodbye to friends near and far
Not for the wedding but before crossing the bar
Two beautiful young women in heaven will reside
Both becoming angels in white instead of a bride.

ABOUT THE AUTHOR

*B*arbara "Bobbi" Harris was a Real Estate Broker and Certified Residential Appraiser when she was called back into the nursing profession by a life changing event. She had a Near Death Experience (NDE) in 1983 that she described in her book *Conversations with Mary: Modern Miracles in An Everyday Life* that was published in 1999. Some of the stories are republished in this book *Manifesting Miracles: True Stories of Extraordinary Coincidences.*

Her nursing career would evolve over the next three decades attaining proficiency as an adolescent psychiatric nurse, and a Certification in the coveted first group of Holistic Nurses in the country bestowed on her because of her body of work by The American Holistic Nurses Association (AHNA). Bobbi is a retired Registered Nurse and Licensed Massage Therapist who earned a Bachelor of Arts and Master of Science degrees.

She taught Energy Healing for decades and has authored *Spiritual Healing* a seminar course. Bobbi is a Reiki Master Teacher and a Certified Natural Health Care Practitioner. She was President of the National Association of Nurse Massage Therapists and led a movement to bring touch back into the nursing profession. She was Chair in Florida of National Conferences for The American Holistic Nurses Association,

(AHNA) The National Association of Nurse Massage Therapists, (NANMT) and the Nurse Healers Professional Association (NHPA).

Her life has been filled with synchronicity that she calls Divine Coincidences. They are events that defy the odds. She has carefully recorded and stored them in her computer files and now presents some of them in her current book *Manifesting Miracles: True Stories of Extraordinary Coincidences.* She is also the author of the book, *Conversations with Mary: Miracles in an Everyday Life,* now out of print. Her articles, short stories and scholarly papers have also been published in numerous nursing publications.

Bobbi is a member of *The Spiritual Writers Network* and *The Academy of American Poets.* She also is the founder of *The Live Poets Society* in Sarasota, Florida. Her poems and short stories have been published in *Finding Our Wings: A Collection of Angelic Short Stories and Poems, 2015, The Peacemakers and The Light Within: A Collection of Peace and Prose, 2016.*